Reading John through Johannine Lenses

Interpreting Johannine Literature

The Interpreting Johannine Literature series is born from the desire of a group of Johannine scholars to bring rigorous study and explicit methodology into the teaching of these New Testament texts and their contexts. This series explores critical and perspectival approaches to the Gospel and Epistles of John. Historical- and literary-critical concerns are often augmented by current interpretive questions. Therefore, both a variety of approaches and critical self-awareness characterize titles in the series. Hermeneutical diversity and precision will continue to shed new light on the multi-faceted content and discourse of the Johannine Literature.

Titles in the Series
Come and Read: Interpretive Approaches to the Gospel of John (2019)
Alicia D. Myers and Lindsey S. Jodrey, eds.
What John Knew and What John Wrote: A Study in John and the Synoptics (2020)
Wendy E. S. North
Follow Me: The Benefits of Discipleship in the Gospel of John (2020)
Mark Zhakevich
Reading John through Johannine Lenses (2021)
Stan Harstine

Reading John through Johannine Lenses

Stan Harstine

LEXINGTON BOOKS/FORTRESS ACADEMIC
Lanham • Boulder • New York • London

Published by Lexington Books/Fortress Academic
Lexington Books is an imprint of The Rowman & Littlefield Publishing Group, Inc.
4501 Forbes Boulevard, Suite 200, Lanham, Maryland 20706
www.rowman.com

86-90 Paul Street, London EC2A 4NE, United Kingdom

Copyright © 2022 by The Rowman & Littlefield Publishing Group, Inc.

All rights reserved. No part of this book may be reproduced in any form or by any electronic or mechanical means, including information storage and retrieval systems, without written permission from the publisher, except by a reviewer who may quote passages in a review.

British Library Cataloguing in Publication Information Available

Library of Congress Cataloging-in-Publication Data

Names: Harstine, Stan, author.
Title: Reading John through Johannine lenses / Stan Harstine.
Description: Lanham, Maryland : Lexington Books/Fortress Academic, [2022] | Series: Interpreting Johannine literature | Includes bibliographical references and index. | Summary: "In this book, Stan Harstine examines three passages in the Gospel of John in order to illustrate how diachronic and synchronic methodological approaches produce distinct results. Using Leitwörter from the gospel's opening verses to shape an interpretive lens, Harstine identifies these passages as crucial transition points in the plot of the Gospel"—Provided by publisher.
Identifiers: LCCN 2021047092 (print) | LCCN 2021047093 (ebook) |
  ISBN 9781978712935 (cloth) | ISBN 9781978712959 (paper) |
  ISBN 9781978712942 (epub)
Subjects: LCSH: Bible. John—Criticism, interpretation, etc. |
  Bible. Epistles of John—Criticism, interpretation, etc.
Classification: LCC BS2615.52 .H375 2022 (print) | LCC BS2615.52 (ebook) |
  DDC 226.5/06—dc23/eng/20211001
LC record available at https://lccn.loc.gov/2021047092
LC ebook record available at https://lccn.loc.gov/2021047093

♾️™ The paper used in this publication meets the minimum requirements of American National Standard for Information Sciences—Permanence of Paper for Printed Library Materials, ANSI/NISO Z39.48-1992.

*To my grandsons, John and Lewis.
They provide me an entirely new perspective on the value
of passing stories down to a future generation.*

Contents

Table	ix
Acknowledgments	xi
Abbreviations	xiii
1 Identifying Johannine Lenses in the Prologue	1
2 Reading John with Two Thematic Lenses	23
3 Viewing John 5 through Assorted Lenses	39
4 Viewing John 12 through Assorted Lenses	55
5 Viewing John 17 through Assorted Lenses	75
6 Closing Observations	103
Bibliography	113
Author Index	123
Scripture Index	125
About the Author	129

Table

Table 1.1   Occurrences of Select Themes in the Gospel of John   16

Acknowledgments

Bringing an academic book into existence requires a team effort. The support of many individuals was necessary in order for me to locate and retrieve resources needed for this project from my faculty position at a small university in the Midwest. Additional arrangements provided me time away from the obligations of a heavy teaching load in order to focus on this project.

I wish to thank the Friends University Board of Trustees, President Amy Bragg Carey, Vice President Jasper Lesage, Academic Dean Ken Stoltzfus, and Division Chair Jeremy Gallegos for supporting and approving my sabbatical request for the fall semester of 2019. Without this time solely devoted to research, this volume might never have found its physical substance. The Edmund Stanley Library staff, under the leadership of Anne Crane, were instrumental in acquiring a vast number of resources through their Interlibrary Loan Department. Especially, I wish to thank Kristie Sojka and Heather Powell for their efficiency in keeping me well supplied with research materials. Administrative support provided by Bonnie Dexter and Morgyn Rasbury freed me to focus on my research. The technical and artistic acumen of my colleagues Mickey Shannon, Aaron Krone, and Kassia Waggoner assured that the cover artwork represents the theme of using Johannine lenses.

Neil Elliott and others at Lexington Books/Fortress Academic were gracious in their support for publishing this volume, even though they spent most of 2020 with furloughed staff and other national distractions. Discussions for this volume were first held in a small conference room at the National Meeting of the Society of Biblical Literature in 2017. Two colleagues specializing in Johannine Literature, Sherri Brown and Lindsey S. Jodrey, encouraged me to pursue my project with this publisher. Their encouragement for "what could be" provided me a vision for the scope of this manuscript.

David Gibbs has been gracious as my pastor for nearly twenty years to listen to me attempt to articulate a variety of ideas and insights from my studies. Conversations over the past decades with my three sons, Matt, Nate, and Ben, helped me verbalize these Johannine threads in nonacademic language. Most importantly, my wife Deb allowed me to occupy a vast territory on our dining room table and in our guest bedroom with my numerous books for many months without complaint. Without her support and encouragement this project would not have been possible.

Abbreviations

BD	Beloved Disciple
BDAG	Danker, Frederick W., Walter Bauer, William F. Arndt, and F. Wilbur Gingrich. *Greek-English Lexicon of the New Testament and Other Early Christian Literature.* 3rd ed. Chicago: University of Chicago Press, 2000.
CE	Common Era
CEB	Common English Bible
ESV	English Standard Version
FD	Farewell Discourse
FG	Fourth Gospel
JB	John the Baptizer
KJV	King James Version
LSJ	Liddell, Henry George, Robert Scott, and Henry Stuart Jones. *A Greek-English Lexicon.* 9th ed. with revised supplement. Oxford: Clarendon, 1996.
LXX	The Septuagint, a translation of the Old Testament into Greek
NA[28]	*Novum Testamentum Graece*, Nestle-Aland, 28th ed.
NAS95	New American Standard Bible, 1995 edition
NIV	New International Version
NRSV	New Revised Standard Version
POV	Point of View
UBS[5]	*The Greek New Testament*, United Bible Societies, 5th ed.

Chapter 1

Identifying Johannine Lenses in the Prologue

In the 2004 movie *National Treasure*, Benjamin Franklin Gates, played by Nicholas Cage, successfully steals the Declaration of Independence in order to solve a mystery. Only after he gains access to a pair of spectacles with multicolored lenses from the eighteenth century does the document release its hidden secret.[1] The hero must utilize the correct combination of filters in order to solve the riddle. The Fourth Gospel (FG) is often understood to contain a variety of riddles, statements that hold a hidden meaning. Gregory the Great described the mysterious depth of this Gospel as a river where lambs can wade and elephants can swim.[2] In order to comprehend or unravel a riddle, the problem solver must find a way to gain the proper perspective. In other words, she or he must put on glasses containing multicolored lenses.

This chapter will illustrate how two sets of lenses, the diachronic and the synchronic, guide scholarly approaches to studying the Gospel of John through recent history and affect both the questions addressed through research and the resulting solutions. These two different approaches employ diverse filters. Those lenses we apply most naturally often receive little conscious attention in our quest to find the one and only correct answer for a question. Yet, as this chapter demonstrates, the filter selected directly affects how a person views the material by limiting or broadening their range of sight. Since many readers of the Gospel of John subconsciously place a specific filter over the words they read, their results are automatically skewed in a direction predetermined by the color of the lens used.

The descriptions in the next section function in a manner similar to spotlights with various color schemes, filtered light waves which accentuate distinct colors and hues contained in this Gospel. The emphases taken by these approaches to the prologue become significant because they represent the first filter placed over this Gospel's account of Jesus's words and life. After identifying the effects created by these various approaches, later chapters will examine how these same lenses influence understanding at transitional points in the Gospel located in chapters 5, 12, and 17.

VARIOUS APPROACHES TO THE PROLOGUE

Numerous methodologies have been used to examine the prologue to this Gospel. Since the nineteenth century, scholars have proposed historical, source-critical, form-critical, redaction-critical, literary, narrative, and rhetorical methods, as well as numerous others which have emerged in the past two decades. The purpose of this section is to identify the effect various approaches have on interpreting Jn 1:1–18, which is frequently called the prologue to the Gospel of John. These diverse methods employ approaches differentiated primarily by their perspective on the passing of time. Those approaches which investigate the development of the Gospel materials over time are assigned the chronological term *diachronic*, meaning "through time." These include approaches which examine the origins or sources of the material, the likely use of materials from Matthew, Mark, and Luke, as well as cultural influences on the Gospel text. Other approaches examine the text as it exists currently. Their emphasis on investigating a finalized form results in the description *synchronic*, which means "at the same time," as in synchronize your watches.[3]

Conclusions reached by these two chronological viewpoints often clash. Occasionally the interpretations appear to derive from two, totally different texts. At other times these two chronological lenses find similar outcomes and appear to reinforce one another. This section seeks to identify, albeit with broad strokes, some key findings resulting from these two viewpoints. While a discussion of this sort does provide a brief historical overview, no attempt is made to be exhaustive in discussing any of these approaches.[4]

Selected Diachronic Approaches

One early approach to the prologue self-identifies as the literary approach, although the methods employed are not what current literary methods use. The early efforts in this regard sought to examine apparent connections, verbally and in thought, to the opening of the book of Genesis. The first two words of the Gospel of John in Greek, *en archē*, are identical to the opening of the Greek text of Genesis in the translation known as the Septuagint. Using this particular lens, many scholars explain various images and symbolic meaning the FG imports into its narrative by means of the phrase "in the beginning." This method of Jewish exegesis follows the same trajectory on Genesis as wisdom traditions from the Hebrew Bible and other early Jewish wisdom writings.[5] The emphasis found on life in the creation account forms the basis for a primary motif in this Gospel.[6]

The poetic state present in some of these verses led many scholars to suggest they originated in an early Christian composition used during worship meetings. Original proposals suggested this hymn derived from a Hellenistic influence, but more recently some scholars view the source as a Jewish hymn.[7] Scholars continue to debate whether Jewish or Hellenistic origins best account for this particular section.[8] One variation suggests this content represents Jewish midrash (i.e., commentary) instead of a hymn.[9] Since the entire eighteen verses are not stylistically poetic, several scholars focus on the prose insertions centered around the individual identified simply as John but better known as John the Baptist.[10]

Another identifying characteristic of the diachronic perspective understands the text to have developed through various iterations or editions. How did this portion of the text of the FG come to be in its current form? In one approach scholars identify elements from these eighteen verses as poetry or prose and separate them from each other. They identify these disparate elements as additions to a shorter, original composition. In the larger Gospel such investigations focus on locations in the text, which appear to represent a temporal transition. Such anomalies are seen to identify where an omniscient viewpoint is present or where the chronology does not flow smoothly through several chapters. One such approach identifies those portions of the Gospel which derive from "the disciple whom Jesus loved," a figure who has been named "the Beloved Disciple" (BD). Finishing touches were then made by an editor(s). Other theories identify additional stages of development over the course of the first century CE.[11]

A final example to highlight diachronic approaches to this Gospel account occurs in the realm of what is formally known as textual criticism, the analysis of the various papyri, manuscripts, and codices on which the Gospel text appears. As a result of recent analysis some scholars are suggesting different parameters for the prologue. Scholars have already proposed that the prologue derives from an external source, contains a prosaic and poetic divide, or various editions preceded the current Gospel. This recent suggestion identifies the actual prologue as Jn 1:1–5. One basis for this reduced prologue finds support in evidence provided by ancient manuscripts and early lectionaries, which indicate places where early individuals making copies of the Gospel included breaks in the flow of the text.[12] A further proposal accentuates the striking similarity to Gen 1:1–5 including the use of light and life as motifs so that the shorter version of the prologue promotes the "salvific work of Christ as a new creation."[13]

Selected Synchronic Approaches

Methodologies based on a synchronic perspective of the text incorporate distinctive strategies for studying the prologue. Biblical scholars adopted techniques from literary scholarship as their model for examining the prologue and subsequently the Gospel of John as a whole. These various lenses provide additional understanding of the Gospel text and how it tells its story. Three aspects of this approach to the Gospel provide the framework for discussing these various approaches: structural analysis, literary approaches, and narrative approaches.

Structural Analysis

Analysis of the FG's structure was among the earliest synchronic approaches to be utilized. Multiple researchers focused on the structure of this Gospel, primarily as an attempt to restore validity to this fourth of the canonical Gospels, one previously written off by Gospel scholarship as nonhistorical or as having little to contribute to understanding the historical Jesus. One approach utilized the Greek technique of "chiasm" and identified a relationship between chapters 1–4 and 5–20.[14] In this scenario Jn 1:1–18 pairs with Jn 20:1–31 as one of five parallel units in the whole structure. David Deeks describes the relationship between them in this manner:

> In other words, the Prologue offers the Incarnation of the pre-existent Word as the proper ground for Christian faith; the final chapter of the Gospel shows how fullness of faith and richness of worship do not depend upon the continued physical presence of the Incarnate One.[15]

These research efforts not merely took place among American scholars but found a foothold among European scholarship as well. One European scholar, Rudolf Schnackenburg, incorporated a discussion of literary criticism by devoting an entire chapter in his commentary to this topic. He explains the basic contrast between the diachronic and synchronic approaches.

> The sharp-sighted criticism which has scrutinized the Gospel chapter by chapter for tensions, contradictions, and "aporias", seems to overlook the fact that the author could have envisioned his task differently from us, that he was not bound to apply the strict rules of logic, continuous development and unimpeachable history in his presentation, and that he could have proceeded in a way strange to us, but adapted to his own form of thought and kerygmatic intention. . . . This explains why so many exegetes are now skeptical with regard to all efforts to find a "better" order by transposing either large blocks or small elements of the

text, and prefer to do their best with the present arrangement, which they try to show is that of the evangelist.[16]

Regarding the prologue, which was the focus of great attention among historical-critical scholarship during the twentieth century, Schnackenburg notes that interpretation "must follow the actual lines of its structure" because that is how it appears in the version currently available. His opinion does not, however, preclude analysis into the prologue's development.[17]

Literary Approaches

A recently published volume titled *How John Works* contains essays on numerous literary components found in the Gospel of John.[18] While the term *literary criticism* can indicate a broad spectrum of approaches, this section highlights efforts examining this text as a complete piece of literature and what might be understood from such an approach. Identifying clues to the genre is primary among these many possible approaches.

Handbooks on rhetoric written by classical Greek and Latin authors have been mined for useful elements to help understand ancient perceptions of genre. One such analysis examines the prologue and what *peristaseis* (circumstances) are provided as clues toward describing the genre of the FG. Once identified, "these generic cues create a pathway for meaning for a text, thereby shaping and constraining its reading and interpretation."[19] In other words, rather than looking at this Gospel as a collection of stories developed over the decades since Jesus's life and ministry, this Gospel can be viewed as an intentional narrative which provides its reader clues toward the author's goal. These *peristaseis* are useful for identifying what this writing is not as much as what it is.[20] A reader informed by the world of classical literature would recognize that "the rest of the story is going to be about the further adventures of the Word" as introduced in the prologue.[21]

While genre recognition provides one crucial lens for examining any of the canonical Gospels, various proposals exist on the nature and the specifics of genre. Arguments are made for the Gospel's genre as a whole and for "micro-genres" at various places in the Gospel. One such micro-genre identifies John as an exegetical narrative.[22] This viewpoint identifies the prologue's genre, as does Douglas Estes earlier, but in this case highlights similarities found in contemporary Jewish narratives. Through this cultural lens the prologue establishes "a narrative arc that extends from Genesis to Exodus, from the theme of creation to the theme of Sinaitic revelation and divine encounter."[23] This approach leads Ruth Sheridan to recognize the prologue "programmatically" defining an identity for the community on the basis of these older narratives.[24]

A final example of a literary approach to the FG as a whole identifies the type of medium this writing represents. Research has recently highlighted oral versus written media used for communication and identified distinctions between these two. Such distinctions are critical for properly understanding the text. "Unless we are self-conscious about first-century orality, we are likely to bring our own print-based Western understandings to the texts still extant from antiquity."[25] Many diachronic approaches used for studying the canonical Gospels demonstrate such "print-based" assumptions. Even more importantly, assumptions formed by a post-Gutenberg relationship with the printed medium do not, nor can they, fully take into consideration the view of texts in antiquity when they were copied by hand.[26] One emphasis for literary studies lies in describing the interaction between author and audience. How does the author communicate? How does the audience understand the author's words? Many idiosyncrasies and disruptions to the text noticed by a print-based mentality are simply overlooked in an oral situation, particularly "narrative inconsistencies and even theological tensions."[27]

These examples of literary approaches to the FG and to its prologue do not depend on finding the prehistory of the text, rather they seek to understand the effect and impact of the writing itself. As lenses exhibiting a different hue, they provide insight into the text while at the same time they challenge unspoken suppositions brought by students of the Gospel of John. These literary efforts present a meta-cognitive view of the text, seeking to explore not merely how these materials came to be included within the borders of John 1–21 but rather how those borders are now shaped and understood. I turn now to a third synchronic method, which examines the interior workings of the text.

Narrative Approaches

Narrative criticism can be characterized as a subset of literary criticism. In this approach scholars seek to identify how the Gospel functions by examining plot development, characterization, point of view, and other categories associated with narratives. This sphere of analysis encompasses the prologue when scholars, at least for their narrative analysis, consider it integral to the form we now have for the Gospel of John.[28]

One specific perspective examines recognition scenes in the FG in order to focus attention on how the reader evaluates and responds to characters in the Gospel as they recognize Jesus. The prologue forms a crucial foundation for this study.

> From the very starting point, the prologue orchestrates an eureka moment for the reader by means of its riddle structure. The reader is introduced to a series

of undefined roles and pronouns and is kept in suspense until the final exposure of the proper name. The reader's anagnorisis [recognition] takes place in the prologue.[29]

Kasper Bro Larsen clarifies that the prologue prepares both those hearing the story read and those reading it aloud for others to be brought into the same "reciprocal recognition narrative of God and man" as the FG presents.[30] The value of the prologue's contribution to the entire Gospel is such that avoiding or eliminating it would negatively impact the Gospel's effect on its readers.

Using a synchronic time frame for research does not dismiss the issues raised by studies on the developmental stages of the FG. Indeed, many discussions of the prologue take such textual factors into account.[31] Diachronic approaches to the prologue often emphasize disruptions to the flow of the text and identify multiple authors as the primary explanation for their existence. However, analyzing these same locations through a synchronic lens suggests "the prologue as a whole gives its narrator's point of view on the one who will be the central character in his narrative."[32] Indeed, the prologue does not provide a single perspective regarding Jesus's identity but functions as "a confession on the part of the narrator and the community of believers he represents."[33] Such perspective on the point of view of the individual narrator or evangelist is not restricted to the prologue; it can also be found at key points in the fuller narrative.

A third approach considers the impact of characterization as it relates to understanding the text.[34] A character develops various qualities as he or she appears in various scenes of the narrative. Some individual characters or even groups appear in the text on more than one occasion, often expanding their character qualities with each scene. For instance, Jesus's early disciples assign distinct titles to Jesus as each one encounters him.[35] "Rabbi" is succeeded by "Messiah" and "the one about whom Moses wrote" is replaced by "Son of God" or "King of Israel." Character development for two important figures, John the Baptist and Jesus, begins in the prologue. Despite numerous appearances by Jesus throughout the Gospel narrative, the prologue remains "the greatest source of direct information about Jesus."[36] The contribution to character development within the prologue informs both those who read the Gospel and those who hear it read as they evaluate the diverse manner in which other characters engage with Jesus.[37] For instance, despite their propensity to agree with the identification by Nathanael that Jesus is both Son of God and King of Israel, those hearing or reading recognize that even his exalted claim does not fully replicate Jesus's *full* identity as the prologue has described it. Only when Thomas encounters the resurrected Jesus and proclaims, *My Lord and My God*,[38] does any disciple's claim reach such clarity.

RELATIONSHIP TO THE "GOSPEL PROPER"

When not examining the prologue for its own value, scholars often set their sights on determining how the prologue connects with the remainder of the FG. Diachronic methods monopolized discussions into the late 1960s, resulting in a nearly unanimous consensus.

> Certain conclusions are universally accepted. John xxi is clearly an appendix to the Gospel proper.... Further, 1.1–18 is a self-contained section.... Estimates vary as to the closeness of the relation between the Prologue and the bulk of the Gospel.[39]

Structural analysis of the text issued a challenge to the status quo. Deeks identified the prologue as having "the closest possible connexion [sic] with the remainder of the Gospel."[40] Current scholarship may utilize either diachronic or synchronic methods in its analysis of the relationship, and the two often merge in these discussions. The next section will limit its examples to those proposals, which view the prologue as an editorial addition or describe the prologue's connection in functional terms.

The Prologue as an Editorial Addition

The most significant discussion around the existence of multiple editions of the FG is found in the recent work by Urban C. von Wahlde. In his first volume, von Wahlde identifies his various editions of the text using distinct font type settings. Following a diachronic approach, von Wahlde identifies Jn 1:1–18 as entirely derived from an external source with some additions by the editor to incorporate it into the final, that is, his third edition of the FG.[41] As a result von Wahlde emphasizes the prologue cannot be understood until the fuller Gospel is understood.[42] He views this third editor as being more concerned with modifying the FG's theological perspective than in making changes to the larger narrative account.[43]

Andrew Lincoln also proposes a three-stage editing process, although with substantial variations from von Wahlde's process. For Lincoln, the first edition began with the introduction of John the Baptizer (JB) in 1:6. This opening was replaced by the loftier language now present, which incorporated the JB material. Lincoln's second version concludes at 20:31. The third edition incorporated chapter 21 and the witness by the BD. Since Lincoln attributes the first two versions to the same individual, a sense of continuity exists between the prologue and the Gospel, even though the evangelist may have co-opted the prologue's material from elsewhere.[44]

Some scholars see a two-step process in the FG's development.[45] For Paul Anderson, the prologue's importance lies in its preparatory role. The reader who hears this version of the Jesus story is prepared for and brought into a specific mode of interpretation by the opening segment of the FG.[46] Echoing von Wahlde's sentiment, Anderson recognizes "the Gospel needs the Prologue, but the Prologue also needs the Gospel."[47] Because he views the prologue as an addition to the original narrative, the final product merges the worship of those Christians first hearing the Gospel of John into an experience for others who would hear this Gospel read elsewhere. The experiential engagement of worship and knowledge of the story of Jesus is a critical element of the prologue and the Gospel proper.[48]

Others portray the relationship of the prologue with the FG in a developmental manner. Schnackenburg also describes the prologue as a necessary part of the Gospel of John. "In its present form, it is indissolubly linked with the Gospel itself, and it only remains to be asked what is its point as the opening section."[49] Schnackenburg, like Lincoln, recognizes deliberate redaction within this material and attributes these alterations to the evangelist.[50] His analysis characterizes the prologue's contribution as theological because it describes the Incarnation.[51]

Each of these four approaches highlights a difficulty in describing the relationship between prologue and Gospel. Each approach utilizes diachronic methods to examine this relationship. However, not every scholar assumes a developmental process; others assume specific reasons behind the connection and seek to discover them. The next section briefly describes several such approaches.

Defining the Relationship via Purpose

Scholars employ various analogies attempting to communicate the function of the prologue within the Gospel as a whole. One frequently hears a comparison to a modern preface or an author's introduction to a book. Such elements provide an overview or summary of the material which follows.[52] Another description portrays the prologue as an overture to a musical production, whereby major melodic themes from the larger composition are combined to prepare the listener for important strains appearing throughout the opera or movie soundtrack.[53] This section will describe three recent positions taken before clarifying disagreements still existing among scholars in this century.

Several scholars build upon the theological significance of the prologue. Alan Culpepper finds similarities between these two portions of the FG in the form of "five divine initiatives" present in the prologue.[54] As long as the prologue is not extraneous to the Gospel proper, his investigation indicates that "the theological themes and concepts introduced in the prologue and developed subsequently in the Gospel form the core of Johannine thought."⁵⁵ Gail O'Day likewise views the prologue through a theological lens and indicates the evangelist establishes a context for the FG within the larger biblical narrative. She likens the impact of the prologue to a "geological cross section," which presents "the substructure that is at work within and under what is visible on the surface."⁵⁶ The readers learn about the theological nature of the FG by reading or hearing the prologue.

Other scholars approach the FG through the lens of functionality, whether that be the function of characters or emphases promoted via rhetorical techniques. As a result of utilizing synchronic methods, current scholars describe this relationship in terms not often employed by commentators in the previous century. For Alicia Myers, the prologue provides an important introduction of characters, themes, and narrative time.⁵⁷ This preliminary information functions rhetorically to privilege its readers with information not available to those characters participating in the story of Jesus.⁵⁸ John Painter envisions this passage as the evangelist's attempt to "signal to the reader the kind of world in which the following story takes place."⁵⁹ This "appropriate introduction" establishes the "worldview within which the story, told by the Gospel, *works*."⁶⁰ The prologue does not, however, present a static view of the world but one which describes ongoing activity by both humans and God. In the view of Elizabeth Harris, the prologue is "intended to inform the readers (or audiences) in advance about the drama to be unfolded."⁶¹ Christopher Skinner describes the prologue as "an audience-elevating device by providing privileged information,"⁶² which "provides a grid through which to read the entire narrative."⁶³ The Gospel proper focuses on characters who misunderstand Jesus, a practice which forces the reader to return continually to the prologue's perspective in order to understand Jesus, the Word "present at the beginning," correctly. These four examples illustrate different ways the choice of lens(es) initially applied to the Gospel as a whole can impact how the prologue is perceived.

A third approach for clarifying the relationship between prologue and Gospel proper utilizes structural analysis. If a reader grants priority to ancient writing practices, then "the symmetrical shape of the prologue sets the tone for the structure of the narrative to follow."⁶⁴ Jeffrey Staley's analysis demonstrates the Gospel exhibits a fivefold structure, where each section is longer than the previous one. His analysis challenges most outlines provided from a diachronic approach and, in a sense, flips the playing field.⁶⁵ As noted earlier, ancient Greek writing incorporated a style known as chiasm, which can be easily recognized when used in smaller units. Similar patterns with symmetrical elements could also form structural parallelism with a text's larger framework.⁶⁶ Charles Talbert proposes these chiasmuses play an important role for the reader familiar with this ancient compositional strategy. Because Jn 1:1–3 and 1:16–18 are designed as "minor chiasmuses," they prepare the reader to anticipate others within the broader text of the Gospel. The appearance of another chiasmus at 1:29–30 serves to further hone the reader's alertness.[67] The broader structure of the Gospel also demonstrates this characteristic with Jn 1:19–5:47 and 6:1–12:50 forming "two large chiasmuses which are introduced by a chiastically arranged prologue," while John 13–17 also indicates similar construction.[68]

Observations like these derive from using a synchronic approach. Such research often produces new insight even when certain basic assumptions about the Gospel are similar—as in viewing the prologue as a later, editorial addition. Opinions on the relationship between Gospel and prologue can be simple, yet not simplistic. John Ashton outlines the two main problems facing this question: (1) When was the prologue composed? and (2) Which verses, if any, were added to this composition?[69] Solutions for these two simply stated problems are not always harmonious. His own position on the first problem is worth noting:

> I am persuaded that the Prologue was not attached to the Gospel until a recognizable version of this had already been composed (the first edition)—signs, discourses, controversies, passion and resurrection—and that it was added for some other reason than to provide the readers with a guide enabling them to understand all this material.[70]

Jan van der Watt provides a more affirming stance in response to the second of Ashton's problems.

> The two sections are first interpreted individually, each according to its own principles of composition, and are then related to each other in order to illustrate the semantic interaction (for instance, between history and grace). Such exegetical questions as why there are two references to John the Baptist and to the incarnation respectively in the prologue are thus answered. It is also clear that *the prologue makes perfect sense in its present form*.[71]

While recent activities continue to shed new light on questions regarding the relationship of the prologue with the Gospel proper, any ensuing consensus remains unconfirmed. Each scholar approaching this introductory section to the FG brings personal assumptions and reaches conclusions that frequently align with their own starting position. Does a "more probable" solution exist for this canonical conundrum? The next section will describe an alternate route of exploration which may hold such potential.

ANOTHER APPROACH TO THE QUESTION OF UNITY

Various scholars identify thematic relationships appearing throughout the FG. Some present arguments for an ultimate theme for this Gospel, while others merely suggest themes critical for understanding the narrative. Despite the many discussions around themes, as yet none has been utilized sufficiently for connecting the prologue with the Gospel proper. This section will identify several themes found in Jn 1:1–18 and consider whether some might be better candidates for such a proposal.

Repetition and *Leitwörter*

The importance of words reappearing within a narrative is not a recent discovery. In his book on biblical narrative, Robert Alter addresses the significance of repetition. While not the first to address repetition, Alter summarizes repetition's status in the last quarter of this past century: "The reiteration of key-words has been formalized into a prominent convention which is made to play a much more central role in the development of thematic argument than does the repetition of such key-words in other narrative traditions."[72] In these other traditions such words become thematic, that is, they acquire meaning based on their context in the text, both prior to and following a specific occurrence, since later use amplifies a word's prior possibility of meaning. These key words are given the German term *Leitwort* in the singular and *Leitwörter* in the plural.[73] Alter suggests these "word-motifs" occur with greater importance in larger narratives in order to "sustain a thematic development and to establish instructive connections between seemingly disparate episodes."[74] Thus, detecting repetition proves critical in order for a reader or hearer to understand an ancient narrative. Repetition occurs on various levels within the text's original language, levels often undetected when reading from a translation.[75]

Not only must a scholar consider ancient narrative accounts from the perspective of techniques used during the time of composition, one must also contemplate the oral medium for understanding the nature of ancient texts we currently possess.[76] Since the ancient world's systems for communication were infused with orality, basic tenets of oral communication "undergirded all composition, performance, and reception of texts."[77] With the advent of the printing press, written texts and the subsequent means for mass production supplanted the oral mode. These distinctions become especially obvious when a modern reader encounters a text written in antiquity. Accordingly, a reader who seeks to understand the Gospel of John, and other biblical narratives as well, must consciously engage various techniques used in oral communication.[78] Joanna Dewey provides five characteristics of oral performance, the third of which becomes pertinent in this current discussion of themes.

> Third, oral literature consists of the *many*; happenings are placed side by side, not integrated with one another. For this reason, the structure of oral stories tends to be additive rather than subordinating. The normal way of connecting clauses, sentences, and whole episodes is paratactic, stacking them together with simple formulas like "and," "and next," "and then." Material is not organized in cause/effect or chronological patterns but rather in symmetrical clusters that use simple parallelism (abc//abc), chiastic parallelism (abc//cba), and concentric structures (abcdcba). For this reason, oral styles often appear redundant or copious to our print sensibilities, focusing on repetition with variations.[79]

Scholars using a diachronic method seek to detect older source material by observing disruption to the written flow of the text. This procedure applies a modern, print-based thought pattern indiscriminately onto an ancient, oral-media based text. Ancient readers, as well as those listening to the text being read, were more tolerant of this type of inconsistency and tension than modern readers.[80] In fact, in antiquity, imperfection of form was an idealized practice. Symmetry, especially the type of perfect symmetry a modern, print-based reader might anticipate, was not a goal in the ancient world; indeed, the opposite was true. Any adherence to a standard form was expected to exhibit minute variations.[81]

The social sciences also provide new perspective on repetition. Bruce Malina and Richard Rohrbaugh describe the use of key words as a critical feature of "anti-language." An antisociety, which consists of a group of people who provide a "conscious alternative" to their society as a whole, employs anti-language as a means to distinguish itself.[82] Malina and Rohrbaugh identify nine recurring themes throughout this Gospel.[83] Their descriptive model presents a Mediterranean understanding of interaction with the world divided into three zones: emotion-infused thought, self-expressive speech, and purposeful action.[84] Within the FG, repetition reinforces thought processes espoused by the evangelist's own community. The community's way of thinking finds material expression in key words first introduced in the prologue.

Themes and Topics

Themes introduced in the prologue have long created conversation among scholars. The introduction of *Logos* in the first clause of Jn 1:1 and its absence as a title for Jesus after 1:18 have led some to argue for a separate existence for the prologue and the Gospel proper.[85] Dismissing these attempts by late nineteenth- and early twentieth-century scholarship, Rudolf Bultmann claimed the appearance of specific motifs in the prologue actually demonstrates its connection to the Gospel. While some motifs such as light, life, or glory have meaning brought from other spheres or texts, the reader must still engage them as this Gospel employs them.[86] Bultmann is not alone in recognizing the importance of themes, although others nuance thematic significance in different directions.

As mentioned earlier, Culpepper focuses on divine initiatives in the prologue as a "touchstone" for the remainder of the Gospel. He echoes the frequent concern that only someone who understands the Gospel proper can comprehend the prologue. The themes and topics covered throughout are significant because they form "the theological framework that is needed to understand the significance of Jesus' ministry, death, and resurrection as it is understood in the rest of the Gospel, and especially its images, ironies, misunderstandings, and interrelated themes."[87] Themes appearing in the prologue represent key ideas central to the Johannine understanding of Jesus.[88]

Marianne Meye Thompson set her sight on a single theme, light. She recognizes "the references to light in the prologue already express key aspects of the character and function of light in the Gospel."[89] Yet, she identifies light with the person of Jesus. Once this type of correlation occurs, "the vocabulary of comprehension takes on a richer and more complex meaning."[90] Once a reader recognizes that these themes work in tandem to form descriptive elements of the central figure of the Gospel, she or he gains an added dimension for exploring the relationship between prologue and Gospel proper.

Skinner allows the prologue to set "the theological and literary agenda" for the Gospel proper so that this Gospel's implied reader can "comprehend the meaning of Jesus's origin and mission in a way that the characters in the narrative cannot."[91] Larsen likewise views the prologue's contribution through a singular lens, the plot of the Gospel. After identifying the main question under consideration, "Is Jesus really the one he claims to be?," he notes this concern is raised initially in the prologue and "thematized in the story-world in various ways."[92]

The importance of these prologue-appearing themes gains support from various angles and perspectives.[93] Whether one searches for evidence of literary connection between prologue and Gospel proper or focuses on a singular quality within the Gospel, one common denominator arises: the first eighteen verses of John's Gospel. Not every motif raised in Johannine scholarship can be properly or adequately assessed in this short section. Numerous themes are frequently mentioned; these will receive attention. However, before identifying these key themes, voice must be given to the lack of unanimity regarding this thematic approach.

Anti-Thematic Approach

Not every scholar recognizes thematic similarities between the prologue and Gospel proper as significant. Indeed, some distinguish between these two in terms of their authorship and community of origin. Ashton challenges the thesis that the prologue was intentionally composed by the evangelist as the preface to the Gospel.[94] Using as his foil an argument made by Jean Zumstein regarding the connections between these two writings, Ashton claims Zumstein makes no distinction between terms which appear in both the prologue and the Gospel proper and those terms which are not contained in both parts.

> This is important, because if—the very point at issue—the bulk of the Gospel was composed before the Prologue was added, then it is obviously a mistake to suppose that concepts (and words) found *both* in the original hymn *and* in the Gospel were introduced into the Prologue with the express purpose of fashioning links. They were there already. Moreover, the terms involved here are among the most significant of all: life, light, knowledge, truth, glory, and possibly the light/darkness antithesis too.[95]

Such an opposing argument does highlight the distinction between diachronic and synchronic approaches. Should evidence be found (and I wish to emphasize that such evidence is not yet available) to substantiate the hypothesis that an editor of the Gospel took an as-to-date-undiscovered Logos hymn, reshaped it, and attached it to an as-to-date-undiscovered copy of only the Gospel proper, then Ashton's point is accurate. Both approaches make assumptions regarding the origin of this text, which prove integral to their investigation. Scholars base their personal assumptions concerning the FG, which they often voice at the beginning of their writing, on pieces of disparate information assembled into a somewhat coherent whole.[96]

Key Themes and Synonyms

Numerous themes within the prologue have prominence in the FG. Bultmann's preliminary list provides an appropriate starting point:

- life
- light
- glory
- truth
- the antithetical light-darkness
- the negatives: did not overcome, did not recognize, and did not receive
- the positives: as many as receive, we have seen, and we have received[97]

Eight words appearing in the prologue occur frequently elsewhere in the Gospel. Five are nouns: life (appearing 36 times in the Gospel), light (23), truth (25), word (40), and world (78), while three are verbs: believe (98), receive (54), and testify (33). Acknowledging that a simple word count does not directly infer importance, the theological significance of these words, along with their synonyms, garners them frequent attention. Four of these thematic ideas—word, receive, believe, and life—draw particular notice because they appear in close proximity to each other in chapters 5, 12, and 17 of the FG. Chapters 3–5 of this book explore these sections of the Johannine text from both diachronic and synchronic viewpoints before exploring how the attraction of these terms provides another lens for reading those same segments. The next chapter illustrates how using only two thematic lenses, light and life, can enrich one's encounter with the Gospel of John (table 1.1).

Table 1.1 Occurrences of Select Themes in the Gospel of John

Theme	Total Occurrences	Occurrences in Jn 5:19–47; 12:1–50; 17:1–21
Life (*zōē*)	36	5:24, 26, 29, 39, 40 12:25, 50 17:2, 3
Light (*phōs*)	23	5:35 12:35, 36, 46
Truth (*alētheia*)	25	5:33 17:17, 19
Word (*logos*)	40	5:24, 38 12:38, 48 17:6, 14, 17, 20
World (*kosmos*)	78	12:19, 25, 31, 46, 47 17:4, 6, 9, 11, 13, 15, 16, 18, 21, 23, 25
Receive (*lambanō*)	54	5:34, 41, 43, 44 12:48 17:8
Testify (*martureō*)	33	5:31, 32, 33, 36, 37, 39 12:17
Believe (*pisteuō*)	98	5:24, 38, 44, 46, 47 12:36, 37, 38, 39, 42, 44, 46 17:8, 20, 21

Note: Search for these terms was originally performed in 2009 using Accordance software and version 5.2 of their tagged text based on the *Novum Testamentum Graece*, Nestle-Aland, 27th Edition, prepared by the Institut für neutestamentliche Textforschung Münster/Westfalen, Barbara and Kurt Aland (editors).

Source: Copyright © 1993 by Deutsche Bibelgesellschaft, Stuttgart. Morphological tagging by William D. Mounce and Rex A. Koivisto. Copyright © 2003 William D. Mounce. Copyright © 2009 OakTree Software, Inc.

NOTES

1. *National Treasure*, directed by Jon Turteltaub (Burbank, CA: Walt Disney Pictures, 2004).

2. Gregory the Great, *Moralia*, Epistle 4.18 (Oxford: John Henry Parker and London: J. G. F. and J. Rivington, 1844), 9. Speaking of the Holy Scriptures in general, Gregory notes: "It is, as it were, a kind of river, if I may so liken it, which is both shallow and deep, wherein both the lamb may find a footing, and the elephant float at large." Other writers utilize Gregory's imagery of water and an elephant to describe the FG. http://archive.org/details/moralsonbookofjo18greg/page/n5/mode/2up?view=theater.

3. John C. Stube, *A Graeco-Roman Rhetorical Reading of the Farewell Discourse*, Library of New Testament Studies, 309 (London: T & T Clark, 2006), 2–3, describes this paradigm shift in more detail.

4. The study of the prologue has been represented by several others and little basis exists for me to repeat these other attempts. In addition to the commentaries published in the past hundred years, which discuss various arguments concerning this opening for the Gospel of John, these following writers have included summaries as part of their argument for a specific understanding of an issue within the prologue. Herman Ridderbos, "The Structure and Scope of the Prologue to the Gospel of John," *Novum Testamentum* 8, no. 2–4 (April–October 1966): 180–201, Elizabeth Harris, *Prologue and Gospel: The Theology of the Fourth Evangelist*, Journal for the Study of the New Testament Supplement Series 107 (Sheffield: Sheffield Academic Press, 1994), Jan G. van der Watt, "The Composition of the Prologue of John's Gospel: The Historical Jesus Introducing Divine Grace," *The Westminster Theological Journal* 57, no. 2 (Fall 1995): 311–32, Steven J. Patterson, "The Prologue to the Fourth Gospel and the World of Speculative Jewish Theology," in *Jesus in Johannine Tradition*, eds. Robert T. Fortna and Tom Thatcher (Louisville: Westminster John Knox Press, 2001), 323–32, Martinus C. De Boer, "The Original Prologue to the Gospel of John," *New Testament Studies* 61, no. 4 (October 2015): 448–67, R. Alan Culpepper, "The Prologue as Theological Prolegomenon to the Gospel of John," in *The Prologue of John: Its Literary, Theological, and Philosophical Contexts. Papers Read at the Colloquim Ioanneum 2013*, eds. Jan G. van der Watt, R. Alan Culpepper, and Udo Schnelle. Wissenschaftliche Untersuchungen zum Neuen Testament 359 (Tübingen: Mohr Siebeck, 2016), 3–26, and Sherri Brown, "Beginnings: Introducing the Narrative of the Word through the Prologue of John's Gospel," in *Come and Read: Interpretive Approaches to the Gospel of John*, eds. Alicia D. Myers and Lindsey S. Jodrey (Lanham: Fortress Academic, 2020), 29–41.

5. Peder Borgen, "The Gospel of John and Hellenism: Some Observations," in *Exploring the Gospel of John: In Honor of D. Moody Smith*, eds. R. Alan Culpepper and C. Clifton Black (Louisville: Westminster John Knox Press, 1996), 107–8.

6. Jeannine K. Brown, "Creation's Renewal in the Gospel of John," *Catholic Biblical Quarterly* 72, no. 2 (April 2010): 277–78. Brown sees this as "the ultimate purpose of the Johannine signs."

7. Matthew Gordley, "The Johannine Prologue and Jewish Didactic Hymn Traditions: A New Case for Reading the Prologue as a Hymn," *Journal of Biblical Literature* 128, no. 4 (2009): 781–802.

8. The main voices in this arena follow the work by Peder Borgen, "Observations on the Targumic Character of the Prologue of John," *New Testament Studies* 16, no. 3 (April 1970): 288–95.

9. See, for instance, Daniel Boyarin, "The Gospel of the *Memra*: Jewish Binitarianism and the Prologue to John," *Harvard Theological Review* 93, no. 3 (2001): 243–84, and Ruth Sheridan, "John's Prologue as Exegetical Narrative," in *The Gospel of John as Genre Mosaic*, ed. Kasper Bro Larsen (Göttingen: Vandenhoeck & Ruprecht, 2015), 173–78.

10. For an overview of the issues, see Thomas L. Brodie, *The Gospel According to John: A Literary and Theological Commentary* (New York: Oxford University Press, 1993), 133–37. For discussions of the insertion, see Andrew T. Lincoln, *The Gospel According to Saint John*, Black's New Testament Commentaries 4 (London: Continuum, 2005), 93–109.

11. For proposals, see Lincoln, *Saint John*, Rudolf Schnackenburg, *Das Johannesevangelium*, 3 vols., Herders theologischer Kommentar zum Neuen Testament 4 (Freiburg: Herder, 1971–75), and Urban C. von Wahlde, *The Gospel and Letters of John*, 3 vols., The Eerdmans Critical Commentary (Grand Rapids: Eerdmans, 2010).

12. P. J. Williams, "Not the Prologue of John," *Journal for the Study of the New Testament* 33, no. 4 (June 2011): 375–86.

13. Martinus C. De Boer, "Original," 466.

14. David Deeks, "The Structure of the Fourth Gospel," *New Testament Studies* 15, no. 1 (October 1968): 123.

15. Deeks, "Structure," 125–26.

16. Rudolf Schnackenburg, *The Gospel According to St John*, vol. 1, translated by Kevin Smyth (New York: Seabury Press, 1980), 1:44–45.

17. Schnackenburg, *St John*, 1:48.

18. Douglas Estes and Ruth Sheridan, eds., *How John Works: Storytelling in the Fourth Gospel* (Atlanta: SBL Press, 2016).

19. Douglas Estes, "Rhetorical *Peristaseis* (Circumstances) in the Prologue of John," in *The Gospel of John as Genre Mosaic*, ed. Kasper Bro Larsen (Göttingen: Vandenhoeck & Ruprecht, 2015), 192.

20. Estes, "Peristaseis," 205.

21. Estes, "Peristaseis," 206. In other words the prologue provides "verbal scenery" about the action, characters, and subject matter "preparing the recipients for a true understanding of the state of affairs." Harris, *Prologue and Gospel*, 16.

22. Sheridan, "Exegetical Narrative," 178. Sheridan applies the work of Joshua Levinson to the prologue.

23. Sheridan, "Exegetical Narrative," 183.

24. Sheridan, "Exegetical Narrative," 188.

25. Joanna Dewey, "The Gospel of John in Its Oral-Written Media World," in *Jesus in the Johannine Tradition*, eds. Robert T. Fortna and Tom Thatcher (Louisville: Westminster John Knox Press, 2001), 239.

26. The current explosion of digital-only products would provide a similar comparison when the different viewpoints of generations are taken into account.

27. Dewey, "Media World," 248.

28. A discussion of the prologue's relationship to the remainder of the Gospel will follow in the next section.

29. Kasper Bro Larsen, "The Recognition Scenes and Epistemological Reciprocity in the Fourth Gospel," in *The Gospel of John as Genre Mosaic*, ed. Kasper Bro Larsen (Göttingen: Vandenhoeck & Ruprecht, 2015), 354.

30. Larsen, "Recognition Scenes," 355.

31. Narrative criticism also recognizes other textual issues throughout the Gospel such as the story of the adulterous woman brought to Jesus, Jn 7:53–8:11.

32. Lincoln, *Saint John*, 108.

33. Lincoln, *Saint John*, 109.

34. Stan Harstine, *Moses as a Character in the Fourth Gospel: A Study of Ancient Reading Techniques*, Library of New Testament Studies 229 (Sheffield: Sheffield Academic Press, 2002), Christopher W. Skinner, ed., *Characters and Characterization in the Gospel of John*, Library of New Testament Studies 461 (London: Bloomsbury, 2013), and Steven A. Hunt, D. Francois Tolmie, and Ruben Zimmerman, eds. *Character Studies in the Fourth Gospel*, Wissenschaftliche Untersuchungen Zum Neuen Testament 314 (Tübingen: Mohr Siebeck, 2013).

35. John 1:35–51. The middle of the five disciples mentioned, Peter's confession granting a title for Jesus is delayed until Jn 6:69.

36. Christopher W. Skinner, *John and Thomas—Gospels in Conflict?: Johannine Characterization and the Thomas Question*, Princeton Theological Monograph Series 115 (Eugene: Wipf & Stock, 2009), 37.

37. Skinner, *John and Thomas*, 37.

38. John 20:28, *ho kyrios mou kai ho theos*.

39. Deeks, "Structure," 108.

40. Deeks, "Structure," 110.

41. Urban C. von Wahlde, *The Gospel and Letters of John: Introduction, Analysis, and Reference*, The Eerdmans Critical Commentary (Grand Rapids: Eerdmans, 2010), 1:254 with the text found on 1:561–62.

42. Urban C. von Wahlde, *The Gospel and Letters of John: Commentary on the Gospel of John*, The Eerdmans Critical Commentary (Grand Rapids: Eerdmans, 2010), 2:27.

43. Von Wahlde, *Gospel and Letters*, 1:231.

44. Lincoln, *Saint John*, 51–53.

45. Paul N. Anderson, "On Guessing Points and Naming Stars: Epistemological Origins of John's Christological Tensions," in *The Gospel of John and Christian Theology*, eds. Richard Bauckham and Carl Mosser (Grand Rapids, Eerdmans, 2008), 329.

46. Anderson, "Guessing Points," 329.

47. Anderson, "Guessing Points," 329.

48. Anderson, "Guessing Points," 335–36. Like Anderson, Deeks views this Gospel as grounded in worship, noting it not merely deals with factual information but promotes a religious experience. Deeks, "Structure," 127.

49. Schnackenburg, *St John*, 1:221; *Johannesevangelium*, 1:197.
50. Schnackenburg, *St John*, 1:223; *Johannesevangelium*, 1:199.
51. Schnackenburg, *St John*, 1:224; *Johannesevangelium*, 1:200.
52. F. R. Montgomery Hitchcock, *A Fresh Study of the Fourth Gospel* (London: SPCK, 1911), 21. Hitchcock describes the process as "giving a summary of the positions assumed, or arrived at, or elaborated in the Gospel."
53. Rudolf Bultmann, *The Gospel of John: A Commentary* (Philadelphia: Westminster Press, 1971), 13. Bultmann notes this overture is tasked with "leading the reader out of the commonplace into a new and strange world of sounds and figures, and singling out particular motifs from the action that is now to be unfolded."
54. Culpepper, "Prolegomenon," 4–5.
55. Culpepper, "Prolegomenon," 26.
56. Gail R. O'Day, "The Gospel of John: Reading the Incarnate Word," in *Jesus in Johannine Tradition*, eds. Robert T. Fortna and Tom Thatcher (Louisville: Westminster John Knox Press, 2001), 28.
57. Alicia D. Myers, *Characterizing Jesus: A Rhetorical Analysis on the Fourth Gospel's Use of Scripture in Its Presentation of Jesus*, Library of New Testament Studies 458 (London: Bloomsbury T&T Clark, 2012), 40.
58. Myers, *Characterizing Jesus*, 61.
59. John Painter, "Inclined to God: The Quest for Eternal Life—Bultmannian Hermeneutics and the Theology of the Fourth Gospel," in *Exploring the Gospel of John: In Honor of D. Moody Smith*, eds. R. Alan Culpepper and C. Clifton Black (Louisville: Westminster John Knox Press 1996), 347–48.
60. Painter, "Inclined," 348. Emphasis in the original.
61. Harris, *Prologue and Gospel*, 189.
62. Christopher W. Skinner, "Misunderstanding, Christology, and Johannine Characterization: Reading John's Characters through the Lens of the Prologue," in *Characters and Characterization in the Gospel of John*, ed. Christopher W. Skinner, Library of New Testament Studies 461 (London: Bloomsbury T&T Clark, 2013), 112.
63. Skinner, "Misunderstanding," 126.
64. Jeffrey Lloyd Staley, "The Structure of John's Prologue: Its Implications for the Gospel's Narrative Structure," *The Catholic Biblical Quarterly* 48, no. 2 (April 1986): 242.
65. Staley, "Structure," 262–63.
66. Dewey, "Media World," 245.
67. Charles H. Talbert, "Artistry and Theology: An Analysis of the Architecture of Jn 1:19–5:47," *The Catholic Biblical Quarterly* 32, no. 3 (July 1970): 364–65.
68. Talbert, "Artistry and Theology," 359–60.
69. John Ashton, "Really a Prologue?" in *The Prologue of John: Its Literary, Theological, and Philosophical Contexts. Papers Read at the Colloquim Ioanneum 2013*, eds. Jan G. van der Watt, R. Alan Culpepper, and Udo Schnelle. Wissenschaftliche Untersuchungen Zum Neuen Testament 359 (Tübingen: Mohr Siebeck, 2016), 34–35.
70. Ashton, "Really a Prologue?," 35.
71. Van der Watt, "Composition," Emphasis by this author.

72. Robert Alter, *The Art of Biblical Narrative* (n.p.: Basic Books, 1981), 92.

73. Alter, *Biblical Narrative*, 92. Alter cites Martin Buber and Franz Rosenzweig as the originators of this term.

74. Alter, *Biblical Narrative*, 94.

75. Alter, *Biblical Narrative*, 95–97.

76. Dewey, "Media World," 242.

77. Dewey, "Media World," 243.

78. Dewey, "Media World," 243.

79. Dewey, "Media World," 245.

80. Dewey, "Media World," 248.

81. Talbert, "Artistry and Theology," 362.

82. Bruce J. Malina and Richard L. Rohrbaugh, *Social-Science Commentary on the Gospel of John* (Minneapolis: Augsburg Fortress, 1998), 9.

83. Malina and Rohrbaugh, *Commentary*, 30. The themes are "preexistence of the Word, light of the world, opposition of light and dark, witness/testimony, life, world, glory, the only Son, and no one save the Son has seen God." They note that some of these are "unique to John" whereas others "receive special emphasis" when compared to the remainder of the NT.

84. Malina and Rohrbaugh, *Commentary*, 35. Their model stands distinct from the Greco-Roman body and soul model.

85. Bultmann, *Commentary*, 13. But see the previous argument by Estes at footnote 19.

86. Bultmann, *Commentary*, 13. "The reader brings with him [sic] a certain prior understanding; but he still has to learn how to understand them authentically." See also Alter, *Biblical Narrative*, 92, who notes "in biblical prose, the reiteration of keywords has been formalized into a prominent convention" and plays a more "central role" than in other narratives.

87. Culpepper, "Prolegomenon," 25.

88. Culpepper, "Prolegomenon," 26.

89. Marianne Meye Thompson, "Light (*phōs*): The Philosophical Content of the Term and the Gospel of John," in *The Prologue of John: Its Literary, Theological, and Philosophical Contexts. Papers Read at the Colloquim Ioanneum 2013*, eds. Jan G. van der Watt, R. Alan Culpepper, and Udo Schnelle, Wissenschaftliche Untersuchungen Zum Neuen Testament 359 (Tübingen: Mohr Siebeck, 2016), 278.

90. Thompson, "Light," 282.

91. Skinner, *John and Thomas*, 39.

92. Kasper Bro Larsen, "Plot," in *How John Works: Storytelling in the Fourth Gospel*, eds. Douglas Estes and Ruth Sheridan (Atlanta: SBL Press, 2016), 106.

93. Joel B. Green, *The Gospel of Luke*, New International Commentary on the New Testament (Grand Rapids: Eerdmans, 1997), 33. Since the format of Greco-Roman books did not encourage skim reading, the "opening sentence was crucial for putting those who either read it or heard it read on notice as to what could be expected in the work as a whole."

94. Ashton, "Really a Prologue?" 36–38.

95. Ashton, "Really a Prologue?" 37.
96. John Ashton, *Understanding the Fourth Gospel* (New York: Oxford University Press, 2007), 388.
97. Bultmann, *Commentary*, 13–14.

Chapter 2

Reading John with Two Thematic Lenses

Repetition within a text is necessary for understanding ancient writings from the perspective of their oral production and auditory reception. What would a reading of this Gospel that takes account of this repetition look like? This chapter provides a glimpse by using two closely related themes, life and light. John 1:4 intertwines these two themes with each other, creating nearly synonymous meaning for them in this Gospel: *What the Word brought about was life, now this life was the light for humanity*.[1] However, life and light are unequally balanced in terms of their use within the Gospel. Light receives less attention, yet appears at significant moments while life, specifically eternal life, dominates the story told in the Gospel.

LIGHT AS A THEME IN THE GOSPEL

Any examination of the word *light* in the Gospel of John faces the challenge of determining how the term is to be understood. Should light be taken in its literal, physical manifestation? Should it be read as a metaphor? In other words, does light represent something real, or does light provide an allusion for some abstract quality or idea? Any attempt to read light exclusively in its physical sense quickly runs into trouble, especially when Jesus speaks of himself as the "light of the world." We know that Jesus is the Son but is Jesus also the sun?

The term *light* appears in seven passages outside the prologue.[2] In all but one of those Jesus speaks about this theme in conjunction with its antonym, darkness.[3] When the FG uses light, the intent is to illustrate a positive quality of human existence as opposed to a negative quality. However, usage of an antonymous word pair does not begin at the time of the FG's composition.

Many scholars remind their readers that the beginning of the prologue intentionally recalls the beginning of Genesis. The language of "coming into being" used in John appears in the same grammatical form as the verb in the Septuagint, the Greek Old Testament. Genesis 1:2–3 (LXX) says, "The earth was unseen and unprepared, and darkness was above the great deep abyss, yet God's Spirit carried itself over the water. Then God said, 'Let light be,' and light became." Light and darkness walk hand in hand throughout the Bible. Yet, unlike Genesis which describes a physical reality, the Gospel of John prefers to emphasize light's metaphorical qualities.

Qualities of Light

Given the abundance of metaphorical qualities of light, the thought of an exhaustive analysis could be overwhelming. Instead, there are a few aspects that provide significant meaning for the plot of this Gospel. Some are covered in detail by many writers on the FG, while others have seldom been described. The three qualities for the focus of this section of the chapter are overcoming, preventing stumbling, and lights characteristic as the first element of creation.

Overcoming and Not Being Overcome

Light's qualities, physical or metaphorical, are often described in comparison to what is or is not. This case is true in an early description of light in the FG: "this light shines in darkness, and darkness is unable to put out this light" (Jn 1:5). Just as in the physical spectrum cold is defined as the absence of heat, darkness is defined as the absence of light. One must remove all heat from a physical system to obtain absolute cold and one must remove all light from a physical space in order to obtain absolute darkness—a feat attainable only within a closed and controlled space. The key element in the FG's description of light is found in the verb translated here with the words, "put out." There is considerable discussion regarding the meaning of *katalambanō*, with various suggestions promoted such as "comprehend" (KJV, NAS95), "overcome" (NIV, ESV), or "extinguish" (CEB). A popular Greek-English Lexicon for Christian writings suggests that the meaning falls along the lines of "make something its own" as in "the darkness could not make the light its own." Another option for translating this word describes that period of time when day changes over into night. These ideas would suggest that darkness cannot replace this light.[4]

Behind this depiction in Jn 1:5 may stand some Old Testament imagery, since the image and role of light reflect a distinctive cultural background in the Bible. In the events leading up to the exodus from Egypt, one particular sign from God entailed three days of darkness in the land. Yet, the account found in Ex 10:21–23 indicates that while darkness was covering the land, the children of Israel continued to experience light in their dwellings. Later, as these people departed Egypt, they were led by a pillar of cloud. When the Egyptians followed, the cloud separated the two camps. Even during darkness, the cloud gave light at night.[5] Even in this time of imminent danger, darkness could not extinguish the light illuminating God's people.

Prevent Stumbling

A second characteristic this Gospel provides for light is the ability to help prevent stumbling.

> Are there not twelve hours in a day? When someone walks during the day, they do not stumble because they can see by the light of this world; but if someone walks during the night, they stumble because the light of this world is not with them. (Jn 11:9–10)

The physical meaning of light is quite obvious. When the only light available at night would have been a torch, a small oil lamp, or what the moon and stars provided, walking outside over rocky terrain was a good recipe for sore toes, skinned knees, or sprained ankles. During the daytime, one can see obstacles and dangers while at night, especially when travelling in a strange place, a person might as well be blind.

An element of metaphor exists for this saying as well. A saying by Jesus in John 9 provides insight for better understanding the metaphor. When discussing with his disciples the man born blind, Jesus reminds them of their situation:

> We must engage in the activities of the one who sent me as long as it is day; night is coming when no one will be able to do these activities. As long as I am here in the world, I am the light of the world. (Jn 9:4–5)

Day is the time for activities associated with the light. While Jesus remains in their world, it is daytime.

When one pauses to consider the position in which Jesus finds himself in John 11, this metaphor receives further illumination. The rulers of Jerusalem are not pleased with his activities and are seeking to bring about his physical demise. Jesus left the region of Judea and is staying at a place considered safe by his disciples. Yet, two days after receiving news of Lazarus, Jesus wants to visit a town only about 2.5 kilometers from Jerusalem. The disciples are concerned for his safety—and perhaps for his memory. Yet, since Jesus identifies himself as the light of this world, walking anywhere while Jesus is present should be relatively safe. Being in the night, or metaphorically apart from Jesus, is the truly unsafe place to be.

The question remains, what do walking while the light is available and stumbling have in common? This word for stumbling only occurs once in the FG. However, the Gospels of Matthew and Luke use it as well. They each record the temptation for Jesus to test God and hurl himself off the highest point of the temple. The tempter quotes Ps 91:11–12, which indicates angels will not let Jesus stumble. Matthew also incorporates this word in the conclusion to the Sermon on the Mount, where Jesus discusses the one who is like a house that fell when the rain and wind struck it because he did not act on Jesus's words. A passage in Romans 9 also indicates the Jews stumbled against the stone because they pursued God without using faith like Abraham. It becomes fairly clear that stumbling holds both physical and metaphorical meanings. One can fall while walking or one can fail to act upon the words of Jesus, the Word "present at the beginning with God," and suffer an even worse fate than sore toes, skinned knees, or sprained ankles.

First Element of Creation

The last quality of light that demands our attention at this time is its appearance as the first element of creation itself. Many scholars and students of the FG identify an intertextual reference in the prologue.[6] That is to say, the author asks the reader or listener to remember a saying from a different account or story in order to understand the present words. For instance, when I mention the phrase "May the Force be with you," then I hope you are somewhat familiar with the *Star Wars* movie episodes. If you aren't, then my words may take on any number of unusual interpretations. On one occasion in this chapter, I have already used the phrase "the Word present at the beginning" as a metonym for the Johannine Jesus. This verbal clue asks my reader to remember how Jesus is first introduced in this Gospel.

For anyone unfamiliar with the first book of the Bible, the intertextual references in the prologue hold no value. However, the well-versed individual recognizes the meaning behind these words. When the informed listener hears, "Everything came about through the Word, apart from the Word nothing that exists came about" and then hears, "What the Word brought about was life, now this life was the light for humanity" (Jn 1:34), her or his mind recalls the Genesis 1 account. Indeed, the story being recalled in your mind as you read these words may have already reached the point when God calls the light "day" and the darkness, "night."

The significance of this reference to light can be found by recalling that since the moment God first spoke—that is to say, since the Word at the beginning—light has not ceased to exist. While the earth was without shape and without substance darkness covered the watery abyss. God spoke; light became present. God spoke; darkness no longer dominated this world. God distinguished between the two elements: "day" and "night." At this point Genesis describes a feature of measuring time not practiced by many of us today: "It was evening and it was morning, the first day" (Gen 1:5). Consequently, the Genesis perspective understands that a new day begins with darkness and ends in light. The darkness associated with the setting sun brings a new cycle. But most significantly, light always follows darkness, the light of a new morning shatters the darkness of night. When darkness falls everyone understands it is only temporary. Daylight will return.

The association of darkness, or nighttime as it is frequently identified, with a period of time when individuals ignore Jesus as the light is recognized by many who study this Gospel.[7] For example, Nicodemus comes to Jesus at night,[8] Jesus describes for his disciples that no one can work when night comes,[9] Judas departs at night after he takes the morsel from Jesus,[10] and the disciples fish through the night, yet catch nothing until they see Jesus in the light of day.[11] Unlike the other three Gospels, the FG does not describe darkness falling around Jerusalem at the time of Jesus's crucifixion. Jesus cannot be ignored as the light of the world. Darkness cannot overwhelm this light.

Summary

The physical qualities of light make it an optimal metaphor for communicating what the Word brought into being. Light's two main qualities, overcoming darkness and preventing stumbling, join together in describing essential aspects of the life Jesus provides. When combined with the understanding of light as the first element of creation, thus making it nearly timeless, this Gospel solidly connects Jesus's activities with those of God at the beginning.

LIFE AS A THEME IN THE GOSPEL

The FG uses the Greek word *zōē* (36x) to speak about life, often including the adjective "eternal," *aiōnios* (17x), with it. On several occasions, the word *psychē* is also translated as life.[12] John does not use another Greek word for life, *bios*, from which we derive the study of life, biology. Some distinguish between *zōē* and *bios* by contrasting them with each other. *Bios* is often said to represent the external aspect of life, that is, the manner of one's living. We also derive the word *biography* from it. A biography describes a person's various activities. On the other hand, *zōē* represents the intensive aspect, that is to say, the element distinguishing life from death.[13]

The distinction between these two "modes" for living is crucial—a distinction not easily determined, as indicated by the popular philosophical paradox that you both "are what you do" *and* "do what you are." Some thinkers say there is no difference between the two sayings, while others comment otherwise. The Gospel of John explains this life introduced in the prologue as the light of humanity elsewhere, frequently combining it with *aiōnios*. The adjective "eternal" means "lasting for an age."[14] When added to *zōē* it comes to mean literally "life of the aeons" or "life of the ages," indicating the type of life provided for a period of time. In this case, the period of time corresponds to the rule of God. It is not uncommon for one to hear eternal life described as though it was eternal *bios*, that is to say, a span of time for engaging in external activities. Instead, eternal *zōē* implies living in a way that continues to counteract the effect of mortality. In other words, eternal life means spending time in such a manner that the life which God alone can provide increases its impact on yourself and on those around you.[15]

Qualities of Life

What elements are necessary to sustain human life? Water? Certainly. Oxygen? Of upmost importance. What about sunlight? We typically describe our continued existence using elements that would bring about death should they be taken away. What elements actually enhance our life? What makes us a healthier, more human, human being? Perhaps some vitamins and minerals? How about interaction with other humans? To ask the question another way, what makes us thrive as humans?

Just as life has its own myriad of necessary elements, eternal life does as well. One of the best ways to indicate the importance of the prologue to the Gospel is to examine different ways this Gospel describes the elements provided for humans to thrive.

Water

In his discussion with the woman at the well in John 4, Jesus begins by requesting a drink of water. When Jesus reveals he has his own source of water, he indicates that anyone receiving the water he provides will be refreshed by life eternal. Later, in John 7, during the Festival of Booths or Tabernacles which occurs in the fall season, Jesus stands up in the middle of the crowds gathered in the temple courtyards and invites the thirsty to come to him and drink. As the source of water, Jesus is metaphorically the source of life itself. Once the Gospel indicates Jesus was speaking of the Spirit, it doesn't take much to hear an intertextual reference to the book of Genesis, when the Spirit of God was moving over the surface of the waters.

Bread

As the source for life, Jesus is more than a mere thirst quencher. John 6 reports a miracle of bread provided to a crowd in the Transjordan region—the same side of the Jordan River where those who followed Moses and Joshua ate manna for the last time. A discussion ensues between Jesus and the people who ate the bread he provided. After reminding the people that God, not Moses, provided the manna, Jesus proclaims himself, not once but twice, to be the true bread from heaven, the bread of life. Just as water was, and remains, crucial for humanity's existence, at that time bread served as a staple for life, even though it doesn't remain as crucial in more prosperous regions of the globe currently. As this conversation escalates, Jesus continues to confront his audience with the conclusion that he is the only provider of life, even to the point of using the disturbing language that they must munch on his body and swallow his blood, an image still controversial and disturbing today.[16]

Other Qualities

While abstract images of life-giving water and life-giving bread are easily spoken of and described, they aren't the only images of life provided in this Gospel. In John 5, Jesus heals a man near the temple in Jerusalem. He then becomes involved in a heated discussion with the religious officials, who control the access a common person has to God. Their problem with Jesus appears to be that he chooses to break their strictly observed religious guidelines for Sabbath observance and to provide this unnamed man a different caliber of life. Jesus clarifies for them where this man's new quality of life actually came from.

> I speak truthfully to you, "The one who hears my word and believes the one who sent me possesses life of the ages and does not come to the judgment, rather this one has passed from death into this life of the ages." I speak truthfully to you, "The time is coming, actually it is here now, when those who are dead will hear the voice of the Son of God, and those who hear this voice will live." (Jn 5:24–25)

The life Jesus provides is experienced when someone hears Jesus's voice (i.e., words spoken by the Word) and fully recognizes where those words originate—with the creator of life.[17]

Life Counteracting Death

As mentioned earlier, Jn 1:4 introduces two themes, light and life, in a way to make them nearly synonymous in meaning: "What the Word brought about was life; now this life was the light for humanity." Some difficult discussions surround the structure of the Greek found at the end of Jn 1:3. The question revolves around whether the phrase I translate as "brought about" should be included as the beginning of the sentence that continues into verse 4 or as the ending of the sentence in verse 3. The latter choice provides a shorter rendering for verse 4, something similar to "Life was in him, and this life was humanity's light."[18] In either emphasis, the main meaning remains, namely, life originates in the Word "present at the beginning with God." Just as darkness cannot overcome this light,[19] death cannot overcome the life found in God.

The Gospel of John presents many lengthy accounts of Jesus's life-giving activity: the woman beside the well in John 4, to whom Jesus speaks of living water and eternal life (4:13–14), the healing of the man who can barely move in John 5, the feeding of the multitude in John 6, and the healing of the blind man in John 9. Such colorful stories can cause one to overlook shorter stories appearing in this Gospel. Not every account must receive a major, full-length production; short stories can also convey significant meaning. One such episode is located between Jesus's discussion with the woman beside the well and his healing of the man beside the large pool of water in John 5. This short episode reinforces a key teaching in this Gospel: the true source for life is the divine Word spoken.

> Then Jesus again went to Cana in Galilee where he had made the water become wine. Now there was a certain ruler in Capernaum whose son was growing increasingly weaker. When he heard that Jesus had arrived in Galilee from Judea, he went to him and asked that he come down (to Capernaum) and heal his son, who was about to die.
>
> Jesus replied, "You just won't believe unless you see signs and marvelous things." The ruler replied, "Lord, please come to Capernaum before my son dies." Jesus spoke to him, "Go, your son lives!" The man believed the word which Jesus spoke to him and went. (Jn 4:46–50)

Jesus spoke, the man believed and returned to Capernaum, death's effect upon his son was eliminated, and life enveloped the boy.

A full-length episode found in John 11 displays an even more powerful effect of the life-giving word of Jesus. A message comes to Jesus indicating that Lazarus is suffering from the same condition the young boy endured in Capernaum; Lazarus is growing increasingly weaker. Yet in this episode, Lazarus experiences the full impact of his condition and dies. When Jesus finally arrives, the two sisters remain in the state of mourning that followed his burial several days earlier. However, the life Jesus can provide exceeds every expectation those who had heard him speak had ever considered. Earlier, he had described this life of the ages as "abundant."[20] Jesus does not provide a form of life that can be limited by death. He reinforces this reality to one sister, Martha. "The one who believes in me will live even if she dies, and everyone who lives and trusts me will never die in this age. Do you believe this?" (Jn 11:25b–26). As Jesus stands before the unsealed tomb of Lazarus, he speaks a word of command, "Come out of there, Lazarus!" (Jn 11:43). At those words, the one who had died days earlier walked out of the tomb.

These two accounts present the fullness of meaning found in the prologue, "What the Word brought about was life, now this life was the light for humanity." The life of the ages spoken of so many times by Jesus does not leave room for darkness or the ramifications of death.

Eternal Life

The Gospel of John does not mention the word "life" after 1:4 until chapter 3. At that point, life is attached to the word *eternal*, or as I prefer to translate the phrase, "life of the ages." The FG immediately associates eternal life with belief and emphasizes that relationship by repeating their connection.

> Just as Moses lifted up the image of a snake in the wilderness, the Son of Man must be lifted up in the same fashion, in order that every person who *believes* in him may possess *the life of the ages*. God loved his own in this fashion, he sent his unique Son with the intent that everyone who *is trusting* him should not perish but have *the life of the ages*. For God did not send his Son to his own to judge them, but so that his own might be delivered through the Son. (Jn 3:14–17)

The passage clearly indicates this life of the ages requires Jesus to be lifted up, originates in God's love, and results in a deliverance.

Later in the same chapter, this life of the ages is again explained: "The one who believes in the Son has the life of the ages, but the one who disobeys the Son will not see this life but will see only God's displeasure remaining towards him" (Jn 3:36). Life of the ages is associated with obedience to the Son, by use of a word for disobedience frequently associated with a human response to the divine.[21] The realm for disobedience is one's response to the words of God spoken by the one God sent.

Eternal life is experienced in relationship with belief: a belief demonstrated by obeying the words Jesus speaks. This aspect is reflected in two other sections of this Gospel. In John 5, Jesus speaks to those who are disappointed in his healing of the man outside the temple on the Sabbath:

I speak truthfully to you, "The one who hears my word and believes the one who sent me possesses life of the ages and does not come to the judgment, rather this one has passed from death into this life of the ages." (Jn 5:24)

The leaders engaged in discussion with Jesus seek life of the ages elsewhere, so Jesus attempts to shift their focus and understanding: "You search through the holy writings because you think that life of the ages is contained in them; yet these are the ones giving testimony about me" (Jn 5:39). They don't seem interested in hearing this testimony, as their later response in John 9 illustrates.

John 3 describes judgment as accompanying the failure to believe these words of Jesus. This theme returns in John 12 when Jesus addresses the accelerated attention he receives after bringing Lazarus back from death. He associates his words with the commandment of God while describing the failure to obey either one as equally important: "I know that his commandment is the life of the ages. Therefore, what I say, I say just as my Father spoke" (Jn 12:50). Life of the ages represents the life that the Word brought into being. This form of life is found in the spoken teachings of Jesus, not merely in hearing or reading them but in actually following them.

A contrasting example in John 8 amplifies this focus on belief, obedience, and life. During this tension-filled section of the text, Jesus offers a challenge which only results in more controversy:

> Therefore, Jesus was saying to those among the Judeans who had begun believing him, "If you continue to let my word rest in you, then you truly are my followers and you will know truth, and that truth will set you free." (Jn 8:31–32)

Jesus attempts, to no avail, to persuade those confronting him by reminding them of the need to continue in his teaching in order to experience the life of the ages: "I speak truthfully to you, if anyone keeps my word, he will not experience death in this age" (Jn 8:51).

This life, first introduced in the prologue, is discussed in a variety of ways. It is associated with living water, living bread, and keeping the words of Jesus. Throughout the FG, life may seem to be a symbol with many changing colors. However, such is not the case. Rather, life remains steady although there are many ways to describe it. As Jesus prepares for his arrest, trials, and own physical death, he gives one last insight into this life that has been so integral to the story: "This is eternal life that they might know you, the only true God, and might know the one whom you sent, Jesus Christ" (Jn 17:3). The life "the Word brought about" that is "the light for humanity" is the knowledge of God, the one whom the Word makes known and whom many humans seek to worship in truth and in spirit. Life of the ages truly is from a different realm, truly is life beyond what we ordinarily encounter. Life is not received through the proper working of our digestive system. Life comes to us through the proper working of our auditory system—we hear the Word "present at the beginning with God."

Summary

The Gospel of John describes the life brought about by the Word as life of the ages. Such a description emphasizes an existence diametrically opposed to death's activities. Not only does the Word present at the beginning provide life to address the mortal human condition, it promotes a human existence which challenges the ramifications of mortality at every turn. This life infuses believing humanity with a distinct perspective, one that refuses to see deadness as a finality: whether that be in our existence, our hopes, our dreams, or our relationships. The life presents an alternative to the consequences from the Genesis 3 account of the failure by Adam and Eve to trust God's bountiful provisions. The life now possible restores the availability of these same provisions, perhaps to an even greater degree than were first available. This life is available to those who willingly trust that Jesus's existence was indeed the physical manifestation of God with us, Immanuel.

WHAT IS THE ALTERNATIVE?

This final section takes an approach that is often expected in formal presentations, especially those of the ancient world. What would this Gospel be like without the prologue? How might the message change without this information provided in the opening verses?

Light outside the Prologue

Light does not appear after the prologue until after that most famous section of the FG. What is the reader to make of this concept with no prior knowledge from the prologue?

> For God did not send his Son to his own to judge them, but so that his own might be delivered through the Son. The one believing in him is not being judged; the one not believing in him has been judged already, because they have not believed in the name of the unique son of God. This is the judgment, namely Light has come into the world and humanity loved the darkness more than the Light; for the things they do are evil.

Everyone who carries out the trivial and base things of life hates the Light, and they do not move toward the Light lest their actions be recognized for what they are; But the one who engages in the true things of life moves toward the Light so that their actions might be seen to be done in God's presence. (Jn 3:17–21)

The introduction of light to describe the judgment seems strangely out of place without the prologue's influence. Where did the writer get this "light?" What does "light" refer to? How can one hate the light? These concerns make this passage less certain rather than more certain. The prologue informs the identity of the metaphor so that later in the Gospel the message may be crystal clear.[22]

Twice in this Gospel Jesus states, "I am the world's light."[23] It may be possible to understand previous words on light once Jesus associates himself with the metaphor. Jesus did use a similar analogy in John 6 when he refers to himself as "the bread of life" four times. The association of light with the sun, and in polytheistic cultures with a deity, may not fully account for the depth of meaning in Jesus's words.

The metaphor used by Jesus in John 12 may be even more cryptic without the prologue's information.

Then Jesus spoke to them, "The light is among you for only a short time longer. Walk while you have the light, so that darkness does not put out the light in you; Those who walk surrounded by darkness do not see where they are going. While you have light, believe in the light so you might become sons of light." Jesus said these things and then departing he hid himself from them. (Jn 12:35–36)

What is meant by becoming sons of light? The ancient world included religious movements known as mystery religions because their teachings were not shared with outsiders. Without the prologue, the FG might be understood to share the teachings of a mystery religion, which can only be understood by those who practice it.

Life outside the Prologue

On the other hand, because life is used so often outside the prologue it is more easily interpreted and understood, although not immediately.[24] Eternal life is first referred to in Jn 3:15–16 yet is mentioned as though the audience should already know what it is. Only in Jn 17:3 is eternal life identified with any specific reference, as noted earlier.

Yet, there are places where the teaching of Jesus will be unclear to the reader uninformed by the prologue. In John 5, Jesus compares life with death on the one hand and is more cryptic.

"For as the Father raises the dead, giving them life, so too the Son gives life to whomever he desires." . . . I speak truthfully to you, "The time is coming, actually it is here now, when those who are dead will hear the voice of the Son of God, and those who hear this voice will live. For just as the Father holds life in himself, so too, He has given this same life to the Son so that he holds life in himself." (Jn 5:21, 25–26)

Does the life which Jesus refers to only occur after one dies, as in the example of the Father? Does the life Jesus offers differ from life the Father provides? What life do the Father and Son hold in themselves? When Life reunites with Light in John 8, the opportunity for misreading is again present: "Jesus again spoke to them, 'I am the light of the world, the one who follows me will not walk in darkness but will have the light of life'" (Jn 8:12). How does this light-and-darkness metaphor work? Why would someone go out when it is dark and walk around? What is this "light of life"?

Through the ages many have drawn conclusions and sought to clarify the relationship between life and light. Comparisons have been made with Jewish thought, with Hellenistic thought, and sometimes with writings less well known, some of which merge philosophies of the ancient world. Normally, the question each one seeks to answer is "Why?" Why does the Gospel of John use this language? Why does the FG seek to reframe this language for its own purpose? Seeing an approach from the seventeenth century may help clarify the historic scholastic endeavor.

> [*And the life was the light of men.*] *Life* through Christ was *light* arising in the darkness of man's fall and sin; a *light* by which all believers were to walk. St. John seems in this clause to oppose the *life* and *light* exhibited in the Gospel, to that *life* and *light* which the Jews boasted of in their law. They expected *life* from the works of the law, and they knew no greater *light* than that of the law; which therefore they extol with infinite boasts and praises which they give it.
>
> Take one instance for all: "God said, Let there be *light*. R. Simeon saith, *Light* is written there five times, according to the five parts of the law [i.e. the Pentateuch], and God said, Let there be *light*; according to the book of Genesis, wherein God, busying himself, made the world. And there was *light*; according to the book of Exodus, wherein the Israelites came out of darkness into *light*. And God saw the *light* that it was good; according to the Book of Leviticus, which is filled with rites and ceremonies.
>
> And God divided betwixt the *light* and the darkness; according to the Book of Numbers, which divided betwixt those that went out of Egypt, and those that entered into the land. And God called the *light*, day; according to the Book of Deuteronomy, which is replenished with manifold traditions." A gloss this is upon *light*, full of darkness indeed![25]

Approaches seeking to understand what we don't know in the FG rarely take into account how the remainder of the Gospel uses life and light.

When the prologue is seen as an intentional introduction to the contents of the Gospel of John, many elements that follow can be understood more precisely. When the prologue's material is left out, ignored, or even forgotten while reading the Gospel those reading can encounter difficulty because, like the hero in *National Treasure*, they lack the correct combination of filters to unlock the seemingly mysterious language. The readers may not understand the metaphors used or may even misread what is recorded. The next three chapters will investigate whether an approach similar to the one illustrated in this chapter can examine multiple themes as they interact within the text of the FG.

NOTES

1. Biblical quotations are the author's own translation throughout. Any quotation used from another translation is identified as such.
2. John 3:19–21, 5:35, 8:12, 9:5, 11:9–10, 12:35–36, and 12:46.
3. John 5:35.
4. Frederick W. Danker et al., eds., *Greek-English Lexicon of the New Testament and Other Early Christian Literature* (BDAG) (Chicago: University of Chicago Press, 2000), s.v. "*katalambanō*."
5. Exodus 14:20.
6. Boyarin, "Memra," 26, and Gordley, "Didactic Hymn," 800.
7. For example, Craig S. Keener, *The Gospel of John: A Commentary*, 2 vols. (Peabody, MA: Hendrickson, 2003), 1:382–85, 536.
8. John 3:2.
9. John 9:4.
10. John 13:30.
11. John 21:3.
12. John 10:11, 14, 17, 24*; 12:25, 27*; 13:37; 15:13. Exceptions to "life" marked by asterisk (*).
13. Henry George Liddell, Robert Scott, and Henry Stuart Jones, *A Greek-English Lexicon*, 9th ed. (New York: Oxford University Press, 1996), s.vv. "*zōē*" and "*bios*," Leon Morris, *The Gospel According to Matthew*, Pillar New Testament Commentary (Grand Rapids: Eerdmans, 1992), 463n24 on Matthew 18:8.
14. LSJ, s.v. "*aiōnios*."
15. For more details on the relationship of these two words, see Jan G. van der Watt, "Repetition and Functionality in the Gospel According to John: Some Initial Explorations," in *Repetitions and Variations in the Fourth Gospel: Style, Text, Interpretation*, eds. Gilbert van Belle, Michael Labahn, and Petrus Maritz, Bibliotheca Ephemeridum Theologicarum Lovaniensium 223 (Leuven: Peeters, 2009), 92–94.
16. John 6:53–58.

17. This passage refers to Life five times between John 5:24 and 29.
18. Compare the NAS95, ESV, or NIV with the NRSV translation to see the distinction.
19. John 1:5.
20. John 10:10.
21. BDAG, s.v. *"apeitheō."*
22. 6x in John 1:1–18, 17x in chapters 3–12, and 0x in chapters 13–21.
23. John 8:12, 9:5.
24. 1x in John 1:1–18, 31x in chapters 3–12, and 4x in chapters 13–21.
25. John B. Lightfoot, *A Commentary on the New Testament from the Talmud and Hebraica*, 1658. https://ccel.org/ccel/lightfoot/talmud/talmud.vii.ii.html. Comments on John 1:4. Emphases by the original author.

Chapter 3

Viewing John 5 through Assorted Lenses

The previous chapter demonstrated how reading the Gospel of John through the two themes, light and life, might affect one's understanding. The underlying focus for this chapter and the two which follow accentuates the role repetition plays when one reads an individual passage in the FG. Since emphases of diachronic and synchronic approaches to the biblical text vary passage by passage, these three chapters explore how different methods treat John 5, 12, and 17. Each chapter is organized around a survey of three common approaches: historical, narrative, and rhetorical. After clarifying each approach's unique contributions, the same passage will be evaluated using lenses colored by themes identified from the prologue.

DIACHRONIC APPROACH: HISTORICAL CRITICISM

The most common approach over the past century explores what can be determined with regard to the setting, culture, and development of the manuscript under consideration. Four elements from this approach rise to the surface when looking at studies on John 5. A primary concern makes decisions about the original text. A second identifies which cultural background might best be utilized for understanding the text. The third concern discusses first-century teachings around keeping the Sabbath. Finally, archaeological and geographical concerns are brought to the surface. These four approaches form a mosaic for reading the text through the lens formed by historical-critical questions.

Textual Issues

The first principle for interpreting a New Testament writing is to establish the actual text to be studied. Ancient manuscripts contain variations which have been documented in modern critical versions of the Greek New Testament.[1] However, in their search to identify the earliest possible rendition of the text, some scholars proposed alterations whereby the text was edited or changed from its original form *prior to* the earliest manuscript evidence. John 5 plays a part in one of the more famous of these speculations. An argument was made that Jn 5:1–47 originally preceded Jn 7:15–24 and followed what we now refer to as Jn 6:1–59.[2] By no means was this conclusion unanimous; rather it has been discounted by many scholars in the decades since.[3]

Cultural Background Issues

Until the past few decades of the twentieth century, scholarship approached the cultural background issue from an either-or mentality. Does this Gospel represent a background in the Jewish culture of its time? Or does the Hellenistic influence provide a greater contribution for appropriately understanding the presentation in the FG? More recently, these discussions have become more nuanced so that a spectrum or sliding scale better represents the discussion on Jewish or Hellenistic cultural influence. On one side of the spectrum, a predominantly Jewish perspective is preferred because we only have documented certainty that John used writings from the Old Testament. After noting numerous similarities expressed in Palestinian and Diasporic Judaism, Peder Borgen proposes that Exodus 33 provides the best background for understanding early elements in this Gospel.[4] Additionally, Jesus's method of presenting his case to the crowd in John 5 reflects interpretation methods practiced at the time by Philo and in later rabbinic writings.[5]

Somewhere in the middle of this spectrum lies a recognition that Hellenism strongly influenced Judaism in the first century CE.[6] This subtle but consistent influence of both culture and writings in Palestine, along with a more tangible influence among Jews living in the Diaspora, could easily explain the appearance of common language and themes in this Gospel without making John more intentionally Hellenistic. The other end of the spectrum views John through a lens predominantly shaped by the Hellenistic world. In one case, the claim by Jesus to perform work that could be performed by God alone would not originate from a mindset protective of a strict monotheistic understanding found in Judaism of that period. Instead, this idea existed near the cultural border, where some "open minded Jews were in contact with movements in paganism."[7] The conclusion reached in Jn 5:18 that Jesus was making himself equal with God found acceptability within the Hellenistic world but represented a viewpoint tantamount to being a rival to God within Judaism.[8]

Understanding Sabbath

The initial conflict between Jesus and the temple leaders is attributed to the fact that he effected this healing during a Sabbath. Modern questions on this topic explore the history behind Jesus's response to the leaders and whether his response promotes novel teaching or reflects contemporary teachings by other rabbis. Interpretations of Gen 2:2–3 in various Jewish traditions from the time period focus on portraying God as always active.[9] Discussions by rabbis present a tradition that God's work never violates the Sabbath, since his abode encompasses all of heaven and earth.[10] Philo of Alexandria's close dialogue with Hellenism gave him opportunity to explain this Sabbath rest in various writings.[11] Jesus was not the only teacher during that time to understand that unless God remains active at all times, "all nature and life would cease to exist."[12]

Archaeological and Geographical Considerations

The pool with five porticoes described in John 5 has only relatively recently been uncovered by archaeological exploration. Consequently, scholars in the early twentieth century possessed no reliable evidence for the pools, causing them to seek meaning for the pools' presence in the account elsewhere. At various times this geographic description was associated with the Pentateuch, Jesus as the Shepherd, baptism, or the "five levels of society" while the water in the pool was identified with the Torah.[13] After these pools were more fully explored by archaeologists, the text began to be interpreted using different approaches. In one scenario, the large pools indicated by the story are identified with some caves in the area where a therapeutic center was active.[14] As a result of associating the pools with a "supposed" pagan healing site, the man healed was identified not as Jewish but as a pagan waiting at the healing center.[15] A counterargument was made once further excavation work in the area identified two larger pools and six smaller pools. The southern of the larger pools served as a *miqveh* and was a Jewish, not pagan, site at the time, where the lame and sick waited for possible healing according to their own traditions, a healing both unofficial and unrecognized by the religious authorities.[16]

From these four various approaches, we recognize that conclusions regarding the text can be drawn and then reassessed once new evidence is uncovered. Occasionally, however, these conclusions fail to acknowledge how a previously held presumption might influence the results, such as the longstanding reference to the FG as a "spiritual" Gospel.[17]

SYNCHRONIC APPROACH: NARRATIVE CRITICISM

Narrative approaches view the text as a completed entity in what is known as its "final form." Scholars utilizing narrative criticism analyze assorted elements of the story: elements like plot development, point of view, or characterization. Prior narrative approaches to John 5 focus on two main areas: structure and characterization. Structural analysis seeks to find connections in the story line between various locations in the Gospel. Characterization approaches include studies on the protagonist, Jesus, on other individuals in the story, whether named or unnamed, and may include a reader's response to these characterizations.

Structural analysis has a long history of use in the study of the Bible. In the mid-1800s scholars were seeking to determine how John 5 was structured.[18] A typical approach views the passage in three sections, vv. 1–18, 19–30, and 31–47.[19] However, other solutions are also proposed, including a two section approach, vv. 1–30 and 31–47[20] or 1–18 and 19–47,[21] or in three scenes with different borders, vv. 1–9, 10–18, and 19–47.[22] The difference between these structural frameworks and a typical outline can be found in the effort to connect the sections thematically with one another and with the larger narrative.

Connections between John 5 and the preceding chapters in the Gospel vary with regard to the topic emphasized. One key theme identified in both John 2–4 and John 5 is water. Jesus replaces water with wine, spirit, and living water in the earlier section; in John 5, Jesus himself replaces the healing property of water. The passage in Jn 5:1–18 can also be connected with a larger episode, Jn 5:1–47, as well as with a larger section, John 5–10.[23] A decidedly different viewpoint understands John 5 to complete a chiastic cycle which begins at Jn 1:19. In this approach, John 5 is divided into two sections which correspond to earlier sections: Jn 5:1–30 with Jn 2:13–22 and Jn 5:31–47 with Jn 1:19–2:11.[24] The appearance by John the Baptist is one indicator for a relationship between the latter pair while the emphasis on Jesus's authority connects the first pair. Connections are also drawn between John 5 and the narrative that follows, especially with regard to a second healing by Jesus on a Sabbath in John 9.[25]

Characterization provides a second application of narrative techniques. Because the miracle story occurs in Jn 5:1–9 and the man who was lame disappears from the story after Jn 5:15, many such studies focus on this early section of the chapter. This anonymous character who encounters Jesus attracts various descriptions. A neutral position views him as the "main character" who shows "little character development."[26] From a slightly unfavorable perspective the man has potential but remains "ignorant" at first with regard to Jesus before "responding unquestioningly" to Jesus's instructions and failing to accept responsibility for carrying his pallet.[27] Another view explains the man's vague characterization "because only his response to Jesus matters in this story."[28]

Many comments portray this man harshly due to his second encounter with Jesus and Jesus's command in 5:15, "do not sin anymore." The field of disability studies provides one such negative portrait. This man who can now walk "rejects the 'otherness' of Jesus and the antisociety for acceptance by the normate society."[29] He never reaches the baptismal waters despite his encounter with Jesus. Once the man leaves Jesus, he goes to the Jews and then disappears from the stage while the Jews enter into dialogue with Jesus. However, a negative approach may not be preferred for understanding his character. Since the man is also presented as "a proclaimer (in good Johannine tradition)" negative portraits may miss "the transitional nature of his role in the narrative."[30]

These examples highlight differences in narrative approaches to the same passage or character. Such distinctions primarily rest in the lenses or themes which dominate the viewpoint of the interpreter. Although a degree of overlapping may exist in the approach and results, conclusions often depend upon the priority granted specific themes or ideas. In other words, the premise underlying each pursuit plays a significant role in determining which conclusions are finally reached by the researcher.

SYNCHRONIC APPROACH: RHETORICAL CRITICISM

Rhetorical approaches to studying the Gospel of John are relatively recent. Rhetorical criticism typically builds upon ancient Greco-Roman rhetorical practices and applies those to the text of the Gospel in order to distinguish and identify persuasive elements in the classical sense. The application of classical Greek and Latin rhetoric to narratives like John 5 does present its own unique challenges.[31] One difficulty when discussing rhetorical approaches appears in defining terminology, as some reader response critics also utilize rhetorical strategies.[32]

Classical rhetorical theory requires an appropriate identification of the text's genre before one can recognize the techniques involved. In this episode, set during an unnamed festival in Jerusalem, charges that the healing by Jesus violated Sabbath practices and his response to that charge suggest a trial or more specifically a forensic situation as the genre.[33] In such a situation the perfect rhetorical presentation would consist of five points, even though Jn 5:19–30 does not present each of them clearly. From this rhetorical vantage point, the reader recognizes Jesus's actions as acceptable for one acting as God's agent.[34] The second discourse section, Jn 5:31–47, portrays Jesus as benevolent and must be analyzed using a different set of techniques.[35] Yet, these rhetorical models remain deficient to a degree for analyzing the passage within the confines of a narrative. Examining these rhetorical devices reveals a text that "mocks the conventions of ordinary rhetoric, subverting the surface structure of argument to push the hearer into an encounter not with words, but with the Word himself."[36]

The element of persuasion provides a crucial perspective for rhetorical approaches. How does a written text persuade its reader? More specifically, how did ancient authors communicate to their readers using stories?[37] Many texts include appeals to an ancient authority in order to substantiate the validity of their claim.[38] Ancient rhetoric provides an appropriate color palette to accentuate the role played by the various witnesses Jesus names in Jn 5:31–47. Alicia Myers notes the importance of one rhetorical device used by ancient writers known as *synkrisis*, which is a comparison of opposite persons.

> Read in this light, the result of Jesus' *synkrisis* between the witnesses of John and that of his Father and Scripture is not so much the degradation of John's testimony—indeed, if John's words were not needed, the evangelist has wasted much space on their inclusion. Indeed, the *synkrisis amplifies* the persuasive power of the testimony from the Father and Scripture. Jesus does not receive John's testimony, not because it is invalid, but because it is superfluous; the words of his Father as spoken by Jesus and through Scripture are sufficient.[39]

In this instance, an appeal to ancient rhetorical practices clarifies what the modern reader might conclude upon hearing that Jesus does "not receive human testimony."[40] Examining the persuasive forces within the text replaces the matter-of-fact viewpoint expressed in many historical approaches and provides a reading of the text as it may affect an informed reader. "From the design of the Gospel and its use of *prosopopoiia*, it is only this audience [those reading or hearing] who has access to the information needed for Jesus's words to be persuasive in John 5."[41] Rhetorical analysis undercuts conclusions made by any approach, which isolates episodes in John's Gospel from one another. Such partitioning renders the text incomprehensible from the ancient perspective.

READING JOHN 5 THROUGH THEMES FROM THE PROLOGUE

Granted that so many different approaches have been used to study the FG and that so many individuals from diverse genders and nationalities have already undertaken this task, does any opportunity remain for a new approach? Can a different approach unveil some element which has not yet been brought into light? The final section in each of these chapters, on John 5, 12, and 17, presents a possible, indeed probable, approach. Specifically, these chapters explore the question, "Does the text itself identify filters that provide additional clarity for understanding its various elements?"

Themes introduced in Jn 1:1–18 appearing most frequently throughout the Gospel are light, truth, testify, life, word, receive, world, and believe.[42] As indicated in table 1.1, with the exception of *world*, each of these terms appears in Jn 5:19–47. Four themes, LIFE, WORD, RECEIVE, and BELIEVE,[43] are significant in all three chapters, thus the focus on them in three chapters in this volume. This chapter provides additional attention to TESTIFY, a theme central in this passage. Before examining how these themes contribute to John 5, it is necessary to explore how these terms have developed or taken on new meaning since the prologue.

Theme Development from 1:18 to 4:42

The phrase in Jn 1:4, "What the Word brought about was life, now this life was the light for humanity," first introduces the reader to the theme LIFE—a life that, however it may be defined later in the FG, originates in the Word become flesh, Jesus Christ. Later the Gospel communicates that the life of the ages (i.e., eternal life) only happens when the Son of Man is lifted up and individuals are believing the Son.[44] Jesus associates life of the ages with the water he provides during his discussion with the woman at the well in Samaria.[45] When he sees inhabitants coming from the city to inspect her claim that he might be the Messiah, Jesus compares them to a field planted earlier which is now harvested with nourishment for life of the ages.[46]

Although many distinguish between "the Word present at the beginning" and words spoken in the Gospel, such disassociation of words by Jesus from "The Word was God" does a disservice to the Gospel's imagery for this theme. An earlier narrative describes Jesus's words as memorable and associates them with believing, especially following his resurrection.[47] During Jesus's trip through the region of Samaria, words about Jesus as well as his own words are attached to believing and then to confessing Jesus as savior of the world.[48]

First attached to gaining an identity as children of God, the theme RECEIVE is connected with receiving the Word present at the beginning and later with the grace abounding beyond grace that comes through Jesus Christ.[49] The conversation with Nicodemus discloses that not everyone receives the testimony of Jesus (or testimony coming from the "we").[50] John the Baptizer reminds his disciples that one can only receive what one has been given from heaven, at which point a reminder is provided for the reader that no one receives Jesus's own testimony.⁵¹ This particular theme carries connotations extremely close to the meanings associated with WORD and BELIEVE.⁵²

It is not surprising that the verb form for "believe" (*pisteuō*), related to the noun we translate "faith" (*pistis*), appears frequently and takes on a significant role in the Gospel of John. What may be unusual is the early dominance of this theme. Prior to John 5, the word *believe* occurs 22 times in the narrative, nearly one-fourth of its total uses. The first appearance links it with testimony given by JB to the light shining in the darkness.⁵³ The second occasion associates believe with receiving the light, with becoming children of God, and with his name, the name provided later in Jn 1:17.⁵⁴ In John 2, this theme describes a response to Jesus. In the first instance, Jesus displays his glory at a wedding and his disciples believe in him.⁵⁵ In the second, the narrator describes Jesus's disciples recalling his words concerning the temple after his resurrection and not believing Scripture and the word of Jesus until that later time.⁵⁶

John 3 presents familiar biblical passages containing this theme. At the end of Jesus's interaction with Nicodemus, BELIEVE again links with RECEIVE. Following a "truly, truly I say" introduction, Nicodemus is described as not receiving Jesus's testimony and not believing the plain things of this world. A comparison between Moses and Jesus, which promptly follows, ties believing with life of the ages and with judgment.⁵⁷ This failure on Nicodemus's part to respond to Jesus's words contrasts sharply with those villagers in Samaria who believe the words Jesus speaks to them.⁵⁸

An additional theme, TESTIFY, relates closely to JB in the early chapters of the FG. Unlike *believe*, which appears only in its verb form, *testify* appears as both a verb (33) and a noun (i.e., *testimony*, 14 times). The prologue describes JB as a man sent from God who appeared in the role of testifying to the Light. The section following the prologue announces a scene change with, "Now this is the testimony of John when . . ."⁵⁹ JB's initial appearance concludes with two statements about the light: the Spirit descended and remained upon a certain man and that man is the Son of God.⁶⁰ JB soon repeats his initial testimony to the religious leaders that he is not the Messiah before the text describes those who do and do not receive the testimony concerning what *he has seen and heard*, namely that God is true.⁶¹ The Samaritan account described earlier also involves this theme. Yet one of the more perplexing statements by Jesus involves TESTIMONY as well. As Jesus and the disciples move north from Samaria into Galilee, the evangelist reports Jesus's statement regarding a prophet's acceptance by his own clan.⁶²

When we examine how these four themes develop prior to John 5, their interrelatedness crystalizes. BELIEVE unites with TESTIFY, RECEIVE, WORD, and LIFE. RECEIVE connects to TESTIFY. These close word associations in the Gospel text develop a field of reference when one hears or reads John 5. Since modern readers frequently partition the text into smaller portions, when they encounter these words they are often limited to a prior understanding which may have little to do with the theme's broader significance. Reminders concerning their portrayal through the FG can provide new lenses on a reading event.

Reading John 5:1–16 with Attention to Themes

During the account of the man's healing, the theme WORD surfaces when Jesus tells the man, "Get up, take your pallet and walk!" Later, this same character tells those questioning him, "The one who made me whole, that guy told me, 'Take your pallet and walk.'" The temple authorities then ask him, "Who is the person who told you, 'take and walk'?" Finally, after the man encounters Jesus a second time, he goes to tell those authorities, "Jesus is the guy who made me whole."[63] A reader tuned into thematic repetition recognizes in this back-and-forth dialogue that Jesus's spoken words are not fully received by all parties. Jesus appears concerned with the man's wholeness. The man emphasizes his healing, that is, his wholeness. The authorities, on the other hand, seem more concerned about the man carrying his pallet through space they control.

Reading John 5:17–18 with Attention to Themes

During his verbal interaction with the temple authorities, Jesus describes his relationship to God as his reason for working. His self-identification appears to cause an increase in the level of their intensity against his action on behalf of the man. Yet, when keeping theme development as a field of reference, the attentive reader recalls JB's testimony that the one he identifies as the Lamb of God is the Son of God.[64] Although the temple authorities might personally be unaware of John's words, representatives from the authorities were present when John confessed that he himself was none of their expected eschatological figures to come. In fact, John indicated to those interrogating him that the figure at the heart of their inquiry was walking among them even now.[65] Consequently, the temple authorities fail to receive Jesus's word a second time. The question remains unclear regarding the man-made-whole's response to Jesus's verbal warning.

Reading John 5:19–30 with Attention to Themes

Reading the FG from the perspective of repetition distinguishes this passage at first, although not for any specific theme. Like Jesus's discussion with Nicodemus, this section also includes three "truly, truly I say" statements. Since a failure to receive colored the Nicodemus episode, this same theme rests just beneath the surface in Jesus's one-sided response to the authorities regarding their rejection of him following his self-identification. In the first "truly, truly I say" Jesus explains his earlier statement about working as the Father works. He identifies the Father's work as giving life to the dead by using the same verb, *egeirō*, Jesus used when he spoke to the man—the only word by Jesus not repeated verbatim by the man or the temple authorities. The second and third "truly, truly" sayings combine life-giving, with the highlighted themes, WORD and BELIEVE.[66] Further echoing his conversation with Nicodemus,[67] Jesus connects LIFE with judgment when he further clarifies the works shared by the Son and the Father.

Reading John 5:31–47 with Attention to Themes

In this section of the chapter, thematic repetition increases in volume to *fortissimo* in the ears of the attuned listener. The defense made by Jesus to the charge that he is making himself equal with God begins with Jesus's own testimony with his own word.[68] In order to better clarify the musical chord sounded herein, the reader must hear each thematic note separately.

LIFE: Jesus associates life with Scripture. Included within this developing frame of reference is the earlier statement that his disciples only remembered what Jesus had said at the temple after the resurrection. At that point in time they believed the Scripture.[69] While his disciples believed Jesus's word, this passage records an opposite reception by those he addresses.

WORD: The first encounter with word comes from the one Jesus calls Father and the Jewish leaders associate with God. Jesus's monologue exists in the form of words. Through his words he charges them with not having God's word in their inner being nor having ever heard God's voice. The introduction of JB as a witness causes the reader to recall both John's testimony about Jesus's baptism and John's (or the narrator's) words when the many were flocking to Jesus, "He gives witness to what he has seen and heard, yet no one receives his testimony."[70] Perhaps even more striking, the next phrase by John (or the narrator) connects TESTIMONY, RECEIVE, and the truth of God, "The one who receives his testimony confirms that God is true."[71] Jesus associates his word with the writings of Moses, last mentioned in the Nicodemus episode, as he highlights the authorities' failure to believe those writings.

RECEIVE: Because the leaders who encounter the man walking around the temple precinct do not receive his healing, indeed, their words do not even acknowledge his healing, this entire monologue by Jesus is framed by a failure to receive. Jesus claims to know that these he addresses do not receive him. They will, however, receive others claiming a religious status.[72] Thematically inspired memory recalls the prologue, specifically, "The Word came to its own people, yet its own people failed to receive this Word."[73]

BELIEVE: Jesus's first statement challenges whether those questioning him believe the Father. He further indicates they do not believe Moses. Finally, Jesus claims they do not believe his own word. Each of these portraits describes a negative reception. Given the positive association believe holds in the earlier portion of this Gospel, an attuned listener would be influenced by the words spoken in Jn 3:18–21, specifically, "the one not believing in him has been judged already, because that one has not believed in the name of the unique son of God."[74] Once brought to mind, this emphasis on judgment recalls for the reader the prior section in John 5, where judgment is based on good and evil deeds.[75] These thematic connections increase the volume carried over from the passage in John 3.

> This is the judgment, namely Light has come into the world and humanity loved the darkness more than the Light; for the things they do are evil. Everyone who carries out the trivial and base things of life hates the Light, and they do not move toward the Light lest their actions be recognized for what they are; But the ones who engage in the true things of life moves toward the Light so that their actions might be seen to be done in God's presence. (Jn 3:19–21)

TESTIFY: The prominence of testimony frequently draws comments, typically using the language of a witness. Jesus testifies, another unidentified individual testifies, JB testifies, Jesus's own works testify, the Father testifies, and Scripture testifies.[76] The temple leaders' response toward Jesus's reply in Jn 5:17–18 enforces the value of testimony. Since they did not believe what JB stated (i.e., earthly things such as Jesus presented in the Nicodemus conversation),[77] nor do they believe what Moses wrote, then how will they believe the witness from one higher than Moses? Jesus amplifies this paradox through his discussion of glory/honor awarded by men or by God.

CONCLUSION

Making the decision to consciously read a text through specific filters affects the perspective one has toward the text. Although a filter made of these highlighted themes in the prologue does not answer many questions brought by historical criticism, narrative approaches, or rhetorical analysis, it does emphasize basic features in the portrait provided by this Gospel. Among the elements identified, the connection between this account and the Nicodemus episode appears to be the most reliable. A second aspect brought into sight is the connection with the early part of the prologue.

Reading Jn 5:19–47 through the filter BELIEVE amplifies the link to John 3. Jesus's three-fold "truly, truly I say" statements elevate this strength of connection. The contrasts between receiving and then believing what Jesus says and the failure by some to receive his words form an evident link. John 3 introduces Nicodemus as a potential seeker, as an individual leader among the Jews, and as a teacher of Israel. He is grounded in the things of the earth and has difficulty making room for understanding the matters of the spirit. Yet, any final judgment concerning his own belief remains ambiguous. John 5 contains no such ambiguity for Jesus's accusers. These leaders, specifically those with the authority to enforce activities within the temple boundaries, are opposed to Jesus. Their main concerns appear to be enforcing behavior appropriate for keeping the Torah instructions and maintaining the ritual purity of the temple grounds. Jesus addresses these various individuals as a single group in his monologue. They do not believe because they do not receive Jesus's word. Even though they fully comprehend what he vocalizes, that he is indeed God, they do not consider his claim valid. Any ambiguity present among the religious leaders after Nicodemus's encounter has now solidified into open hostility toward Jesus.

When a reader considers John 5 through the lenses the prologue provides, these thematic prompts echo the emphases in Jn 1:1–11. These similarities include the status of the Word at the Beginning (1:1), the life this Word brings (1:3), the darkness that does not comprehend the light (1:5), the testimony of John regarding the light (1:6), and the light coming to its own and being rejected (1:11). In one sense, John 5 reflects a partial outline of the prologue. The messages conveyed involve both positive and negative elements. The first claim by Jesus states the positive, he is there to give life to whomever he desires.[78] The second also begins in the positive: that they might honor the Son just as they honor the Father.[79] Only the final phrase in Jn 5:23 introduces a negative idea. Jesus's second "truly, truly" statement also resonates with the positive. His third "truly, truly" proclamation states nothing but positive elements. Unlike Jn 3:16–19, which these three declarations recall to mind, no negative claims are found in this passage. Analysis colored by these thematic lenses clashes with the many others which paint John 5 using a darker palette. As we saw earlier, those studies emphasize that some reject Jesus, others pursue him, while the passage itself reflects a growing desire to rid the region of this man who abrogates the Sabbath teaching. However, using this fivefold thematic lens to read this account of a healing reveals a far more positive tone to the language of this section.

NOTES

1. Among these versions are the Nestle-Aland text, currently in its 28th edition; the United Bible Society text, in its 5th edition; and the SBL edition. Universität Münster, Institut für Neutestamentliche Textforschung, *Nestle-Aland Novum*

Testament Graece, 28th ed. (Peabody, MA: Hendrickson Publishers; Alban Books, 2018), United Bible Societies, *The UBS Greek New Testament: Reader's Edition with Textual Notes*, 5th ed. (Stuttgart: Deutsche Bibelgesellschaft, 2010), and Michael W. Holmes, ed., *The Greek New Testament: SBL Edition* (Atlanta: SBL Press, 2010).

2. Bultmann, *Commentary*, 209 and 237.

3. Albert Power, "The Original Order of St. John's Gospel," *The Catholic Biblical Quarterly* 10, no. 4 (October 1948): 399–405.

4. Borgen, "Observations," 98–101.

5. Borgen, "Observations," 106–07.

6. Raymond Edward Brown, *The Gospel According to John*, Anchor Bible 29 (Garden City, NY: Doubleday, 1966), LVI. Philo of Alexandria is frequently cited as an example of this influence.

7. C. H. Dodd, *The Interpretation of the Fourth Gospel* (New York: Cambridge University Press, 1968), 324.

8. Dodd, *Interpretation*, 325–27.

9. Borgen, "Observations," 107. See also Peder Borgen, *The Gospel of John: More Light from Philo, Paul and Archaeology: The Scriptures, Tradition, Settings, Meaning*, Supplements to Novum Testamentum 154 (Leiden: Brill, 2014), 85; and J. Brown, "Renewal," 285, n. 50. For commentaries, see Bultmann, *Commentary*, 244–47; and Keener, *Commentary*, 1:641–45 to note only two.

10. Dodd, *Interpretation*, 320. Dodd is citing Rabbah Exodus 30.9 and a purported discussion between Gamaliel II, Joshua ben Chananiah, Eliezer ben Azariah, and Aqiba.

11. Cited by Dodd, *Interpretation*, 320–23. See Philo, *On the Cherubim*, 86–90; and *Allegorical Interpretation*, 1.5, where he writes "for God does not cease from creating, since just as it is the nature of fire to burn and of snow to cool, so it is the nature of God to create."

12. R. E. Brown, *John*, 29:217.

13. Bultmann, *Commentary*, 241, n. 8. Bultmann notes these levels of society as "Pharisees, Sadducees, Samaritans, disciples of John, and Essenes."

14. Jerzy Klinger, "Bethesda and the Universality of the Logos," translated by Diana Johnson, *St Vladimir's Theological Quarterly* 27, no. 3 (1983): 171–72. See also Urban C. von Wahlde, "The Pool(s) of Bethesda and the Healing in John 5: A Reappraisal of Research and of the Johannine Text," *Revue Biblique* 116, no. 1 (January 2009): 112–13.

15. Klinger, "Bethesda," 182–84.

16. Von Wahlde, "Bethesda," 132–36.

17. Von Wahlde, "Bethesda," 135.

18. John Forbes, *The Symmetrical Structure of Scripture: The Principles of Scripture Parallelism Exemplified, in an analysis of the Decalogue, the Sermon on the Mount, and other Passages of the Sacred Writings* (Edinburgh, T & T Clark, 1854), 68–82.

19. Francis J. Moloney, *Signs and Shadows: Reading John 5–12* (Minneapolis: Fortress Press, 1996), 2.

20. Deeks, "Structure," 114, and Talbert, "Artistry and Theology," 343.

21. R. Alan Culpepper, "John 5:1–18: A Sample of Narrative-Critical Commentary," in *The Gospel of John as Literature: An Anthology of Twentieth-Century Perspectives*, ed. Mark W. G. Stibbe, trans. Jean-Daniel Kaestli, New Testament Tools and Studies 17 (Leiden: Brill, 1993), 197.

22. Dorothy A. Lee, *The Symbolic Narratives of the Fourth Gospel: The Interplay of Form and Meaning* (Sheffield: JSOT Press, 1994), 101.

23. Culpepper, "John 5:1–18," 196.

24. Talbert, "Artistry and Theology," 343.

25. Lee, *Symbolic Narratives*, 105–6. See also Jeffrey Lloyd Staley, "Stumbling in the Dark, Reaching for the Light: Reading Character in John 5 and 9," *Semeia* 53 (1991): 55–80, and Kerry H. Wynn, "Johannine Healings and the Otherness of Disability," *Perspectives in Religious Studies* 34, no. 1 (Spring 2007): 61–75.

26. Lee, *Symbolic Narratives*, 99.

27. Moloney, *Signs and Shadows*, 5–6.

28. Culpepper, "John 5:1–18," 201.

29. Wynn, "Healings," 69.

30. John Christopher Thomas, "'Stop Sinning Lest Something Worse Come upon You': The Man at the Pool in John 5," *Journal for the Study of the New Testament* 18, no. 59 (January 1996): 19.

31. Harold W. Attridge, "Argumentation in John 5," in *Rhetorical Argumentation in Biblical Texts: Essays from the Lund 2000 Conference*, eds. Anders Eriksson, Thomas H. Olbricht, and Walter Übelacker (Harrisburg, PA: Trinity Press International, 2002), 188.

32. David L. Mealand, "John 5 and the Limits of Rhetorical Criticism," in *Understanding Poets and Prophets: Essays in Honour of George Wishart*, ed. A. Graeme Auld (Sheffield: JSOT Press, 1993), 258.

33. Attridge, "Argumentation," 191. See also Andrew T. Lincoln, *Truth on Trial: The Lawsuit Motif in the Fourth Gospel* (Peabody, MA: Hendrickson, 2000), 73–81. See John 5:10–11 and 15–17.

34. Attridge, "Argumentation," 192–96. See also Talbert, "Artistry and Theology," 362.

35. Attridge, "Argumentation," 196–98.

36. Attridge, "Argumentation," 199. See also Estes, "Peristaseis," 206.

37. Myers, *Characterizing Jesus*, 27–35. Myers applies these rhetorical categories to several discourses of Jesus as she analyzes the role the Scriptures play in the Gospel.

38. Harstine, *Moses*. See chapter 5, "The Function of Homer in Greco-Roman Narratives," 130–59.

39. Myers, *Characterizing Jesus*, 101. Emphasis in the original.

40. John 5:34.

41. Myers, *Characterizing Jesus*, 104. The term *prosopopoiia* refers to the introduction provided for a character who participates through speech in the scene, 51.

42. These terms exclude the names Jesus/God or titles Son/Father. For numerical counts, see the last paragraph in chapter 1.

43. Formatting in SMALL CAPS indicates the term is representing the theme.

44. John 3:15–16 and 36.
45. John 4:14.
46. John 4:35–36.
47. John 2:22.
48. John 4:39–42.
49. John 1:12, 16–17.
50. John 3:11.
51. John 3:27, 32.
52. See John 4:35–36 concerning life. "Since seeing and hearing are both equivalents of believing, testifying to what one has seen and heard is frequently testifying to one's belief." Lincoln, *Truth*, 243.
53. John 1:7.
54. John 1:13.
55. John 2:11.
56. John 2:22.
57. John 3:11–18. See also Bultmann, *Commentary*, 256.
58. John 4:39–42.
59. John 1:6, 15, and 19.
60. John 1:32, 34.
61. John 3:26–33. Some question remains whether these are the words of John or a description by the evangelist.
62. John 4:43–44. "After two days, Jesus went from that place (Samaria) to Galilee; for Jesus himself had testified that a prophet holds no honor within his own hometown."
63. John 5:8, 11, 12 and 15. This translation emphasizes the words that the various parties speak to one another in this scene. The use of "that guy" reinforces the anonymity of Jesus to the man and the temple leaders in the moment.
64. John 1:34.
65. John 1:19–27.
66. John 3:5 and 11.
67. John 3:14–19.
68. John 5:18.
69. John 2:22.
70. John 1:32–34 and 3:32.
71. John 3:33.
72. John 5:43.
73. John 1:11.
74. John 3:18.
75. John 5:29.
76. Lincoln, *Saint John*, 205–6, and Jo-Ann A. Brant, *John*, Paideia: Commentaries on the New Testament (Grand Rapids: Baker Academic, 2011), 107–9.
77. Probably implied here is the concept of earthly things based on Jesus's words in his conversation with Nicodemus.
78. John 5:21.
79. John 5:23.

Chapter 4

Viewing John 12 through Assorted Lenses

Our first excursion into the realm of emphasizing themes focused on a chapter with a relatively straightforward context: a healing and the dialogue that followed. This chapter examines a more complex catalog of events including a foot washing, a messianic entry into Jerusalem, and the arrival of some Greeks requesting to see Jesus. This narrative diversity creates a challenge for discussing the chapter as a unified whole. However, maintaining the pattern of focusing on three common approaches—historical, narrative, and rhetorical—will provide the clarity and structure necessary in order to compare results gleaned from reading the FG through these diachronic and synchronic lenses.

DIACHRONIC APPROACH: HISTORICAL CRITICISM

Historical criticism finds plentiful opportunities for exploration when the story line of John's Gospel reaches this point. Two scenes demonstrate parallels with the synoptic pattern. In addition, a small kernel of a saying may indicate a parable within John, a matter primed for debate on several levels. Finally, the evangelist's increased use of Scripture creates opportunities to explore what one can determine from the evidence available. Five areas form the major framework for this discussion of reading John 12 through the lens of historical criticism.

Organization

Among the challenges facing any scholar of the FG is that of locating proper parameters for each passage. John's uses of repetition, chiasm, and the possible reframing of events recorded in the Synoptics result in both a higher level of difficulty for the reader and more contrasting discussions among scholars. Such discussions typically occur in manuscripts or commentaries, where the author has sufficient time (and pages) to develop the larger framework necessary for explaining his or her content. Basic proposals for outlining this section differ primarily at their starting point, whether that should be understood as Jn 11:1 or some later spot.

Many proposals view chapters 11 and 12 as a continuous unit although differing considerably with regard to the internal structure. Craig Keener identifies Jn 11:1–12:11 as a unit while noting that chapter 12 is highly transitional.[1] Rudolf Bultmann connects Jn 10:54–12:43 while suggesting Jn 11:55–12:33 forms a large subunit.[2] Raymond E. Brown proposes Jn 11:1–12:36 to be the major segment with three subsections in John 12.[3] Rudolf Schnackenburg suggests Jn 11:55–12:36 as the unified section with four subunits in John 12.[4] Andrew Lincoln identifies the unit as Jn 11:1–12:50 and divides John 12 into five elements.[5]

This diversity of opinion on the basic parameters of this passage demonstrates some of the challenges for understanding these events. Does the anointing scene end at 12:8 or 12:11? When does the entry into Jerusalem actually begin, at 12:9 or 12:12? These two examples do not even address the sundry opinions regarding the conclusion to John 12. These subunit breakdowns do, however, provide an opportunity to investigate various understandings of the source material John uses for those elements that echo elements from the Synoptics.

Anointing Scene

While the anointing of Jesus's feet with oil may hold various purposes in the story, that specific discussion will be deferred until the section on narrative criticism. The main challenges this scene faces from a historical perspective lie in determining the source for John's account, how many times Jesus had his feet anointed, and how many different women did so! The conclusions fall into two basic alternatives, either John utilized the accounts found in the Synoptic Gospels or he did not.[6]

The traditional, historical-critical perspective understands the FG's anointing account derives from access to the Gospels of Mark and/or Luke. Bultmann describes the consensus assessment during the mid-twentieth century.

> Since Mark created the literary type of Gospel, to which John's writing also belongs, a direct or indirect acquaintance with the Gospel of Mark must surely be accepted. Such an acquaintance would also presuppose the use of the

Synoptic tradition, as is particularly clear from the Passion story, but also by reason of other narratives and the sayings-tradition.[7]

Bultmann considers other sources were available and consulted as well, including Bultmann's so-named revelation discourses. For this particular element in the FG, Bultmann notes the evangelist edited and enlarged a written source without suggesting what that source might have been. He also proposes one possible explanation for the reversed order of the anointing and entry into Jerusalem; the evangelist's source—which was not a synoptic one—held the two stories in this order.[8]

Some scholars who recognize a synoptic basis for this account hold that both Luke and Mark may have been incorporated. Reflecting Bultmann's opinion to a degree, Schnackenburg suggests the anointing "presupposes a source which the evangelist has used and commented on."[9] After proposing three different solutions to the problem—the evangelist (1) used only oral traditions and independent shaping, (2) knew the Mark narrative and shaped that, and (3) used a written source somehow "related to the synoptics"—Schnackenburg determines there was a pre-Johannine source without indicating its exact relationship to the other canonical Gospels.[10] Lincoln suggests a synoptic relationship is "preferable" to independence.[11] R. E. Brown sees two anointing events as probable with John incorporating elements from the second event, the Lucan account, into his recollection of the first event shared with Mark. For Brown this use does not, however, imply that John used Mark. Rather "the present Johannine narrative gives evidence in some points of being close to the earliest tradition about this incident."[12]

Other scholars hold to the independent tradition of John alluded to by both Bultmann and R. E. Brown. C. H. Dodd challenges the theory of dependence on the synoptic material and proposes the independence of John's material.[13] John's uniqueness can be phrased in various ways. Robert Holst argues for a single incident picked up by the Gospel writers noting that Luke uses a "more primitive version" of the story while Mark and John follow a shared trajectory before separating and adding their own unique Christological aspects.[14] Keener notes John "probably reflects accurate and independent tradition."[15] In either case, dependent or independent, a conclusion to this line of inquiry does not contribute to further clarification of the story; it merely raises questions about similarities and differences between these accounts.

Entry into Jerusalem

The entry of Jesus into Jerusalem presents its own distinct set of questions from the historical-critical tradition.[16] Like conversations around the anointing scene, the main historical-critical concern revolves around the source material and explaining any similarity or dissimilarity with synoptic accounts. Edwin Freed argues the Scriptural quotations provide evidence John was "indebted to the Synoptics."[17] Freed describes this pericope as an insertion of synoptic material into the larger Lazarus story, which then continues with the crowd's testimony in Jn 12:17.[18] Schnackenburg identifies two similarities between John and the Synoptics: a crowd greets Jesus and Jesus rides an animal into Jerusalem. Every other point presents a Johannine deviation from the synoptic story. These distinctions provide him with "considerable confidence" in an independent Johannine source. When combined with evidence from the anointing story, he recognizes the probability increases for an independent Johannine source overlapping synoptic details.[19]

The "Parable"

In discussions regarding the existence of parables in John, many identify Jn 12:24 as a parable, brief though it may be. This specific account about a grain of wheat falling into the earth is not shared elsewhere, although Jesus's accompanying statement about saving and losing one's life is. R. E. Brown notes similarities with synoptic parables in form and implied meaning but recognizes its Johannine distinctiveness. The original source for this saying remains unidentified for him.[20] Schnackenburg refers to it as "an impressive little parable" and finds it structurally similar to, but unparalleled in content with, the Synoptics. Further, he suggests its closest relative is found in Jn 16:21, the saying about a woman in labor. Identifying this parable as "firmly rooted in tradition and catechesis of the primitive church," this saying is probably not a "pre-Johannine variant of the synoptic announcement of Jesus' death."[21] Historical lenses for viewing the biblical accounts profit one seeking similarities and distinctions between the Gospels. However, seldom does this sort of analysis provide a reader any connection between the preceding and following materials.

A Scriptural Quotation in John 12:34?

A fifth and final lens for exploration via the historical-critical model can be found in the pursuit of the likely source for the quotation included at this point. The crowd's objection to Jesus's clarification statements following the "noise" from heaven echoes a Scriptural passage. The question is, which passage? At least seven passages had been suggested as source material prior to W. C. van Unnik proposing Psalm 88 (89):37 (LXX) as better suiting the crowd's statement that "the Christ abides into the ages."[22] Brian McNeil and Bruce Chilton suggest the verse better relates to targums on Isaianic passages rather than a Scriptural source.[23] Gillian Bampfylde identifies a simpler solution, the Masoretic Text of Psalm 61:7, which is "straight from the Old Testament" and "of great authority" as a psalm of David.[24] Such diversity of opinion illuminates the resulting spectrum which occurs once the microscope lens into which one stares achieves its maximum level of magnification power.

When this particular diachronic approach is applied to John 12, source questions appear to override most historical-critical explorations in this passage. The multiple components reduce, if not prevent, any perception of a connected story line. Some elements of the passage receive scant attention from scholars simply because they do not lend themselves naturally to comparison with other Gospel accounts. As a result of the general premises underlying this approach, John 12 can only be described as an assorted conglomeration of disconnected elements.

SYNCHRONIC APPROACH: NARRATIVE CRITICISM

As a means for maintaining consistency within these three exploratory chapters, the assessment of narrative-critical approaches will parallel the last chapter when possible. Because John 12 is composed of these smaller segments, part of this discussion will appear to parallel the historical-critical approach on the surface. The three main topics for consideration will highlight narrative-critical viewpoints on structure, the anointing scene, and characterization.

Structure

Regardless of their chronological approach, scholars researching a passage seek to define parameters for their section of focus. The distinction between narrative and historical approaches normally can be described in terms of interconnectivity. Historical approaches typically view a segment through a lens, which isolates it from other segments within the Gospel while seeking to find relationships to outside sources or forms of the sayings. Narrative approaches frequently seek connection with ideas within the larger text of the Gospel. In this instance, two areas reveal themselves for discussion: general outlines and connecting layers.

Narrative approaches frequently utilize the recognition of parallel structural patterns—identified, in general, with the Greek word *chiasmus*—to identify connections within small passages and larger texts. Charles Talbert locates several patterns of arrangement within the Gospel of John, including chapters 6–12. In his reconstruction, Jn 12:1–50 finds its parallel in Jn 6:1–71. Although at first glance the content in these two chapters may appear unconnected, Talbert notes four similarities between them.[25] Dorothy Lee identifies seven chiastic scenes within Jn 11:1–12:11.[26] Thomas Brodie recognizes two connections between chapters 11 and 12 based on reactions to Jesus "proportioned to the (potential) presence of belief" at the end of four sections and the two prayers by Jesus in 11:41–43 and 12:27–28.[27] Some narrative scholars identify parallels between John 12 and 13,[28] while Colleen Conway further describes this segment as a "pivotal point in the Gospel."[29]

The narrative-critical perspective often seeks to explain the function of a smaller segment within the larger text of the Gospel. Finding connection points within the manuscript as a whole proves helpful for describing how a section actually functions. In addition to thematic repetition, other characteristics draw attention from narrative critics. These connections may be described in terms of chiastic connections as illustrated by Talbert and Lee. At other times shared content identifies these associations. Because John 12 is often designated as a transition between Jesus's public ministry and his passion,[30] it can represent the conclusion of an *inclusio*, which wraps up topics introduced in earlier stories. Alicia Myers identifies elements in John 12 which conclude themes introduced in John 2 or John 6.[31] The temple incident in John 2 incorporates a Scripture citation and a narrative insert of the disciples' memory after Jesus is raised from the dead, while John 6 develops Scriptural themes concerning the Passover.[32] Lincoln identifies the beginning of an *inclusio* with Jn 1:19–27 and JB's use of Isaiah 40:3. Lincoln further identifies Jesus's final statement in 12:50, "Therefore what I say, I say just as my Father spoke," as part of an *inclusio* with the prologue, specifically Jn 1:1, "The Word was at the beginning, the Word was with God, the Word was God."[33] Other sections in John's account of Jesus's public ministry are also suggested as content friendly to John 12: including John 3, 9, 10, and 13.[34]

Anointing Scene

Instead of seeking to identify whether John's account of Jesus's anointing recalls a unique event or incorporates one or more stories from the Synoptics, narrative-critical approaches ask how this event impacts the plot. David Svärd argues Mary's action should be understood as a royal anointing since it shares genre elements with several Old Testament anointings of kings of Israel. The evangelist uses these elements to "refashion" the scene and adapt it to a "serving and dying royal Messiah."[35] Susan Miller, however, identifies the anointing as "a sign of her [Mary's] gratitude to Jesus for the life of her brother."[36] The extravagance identified in Mary's action acknowledges both Jesus as the Messiah and his impending death.[37] Margareta Gruber identifies six characteristics the evangelist accentuates with the anointing scene. One emphasis lies in the unity Jesus's death and resurrection will bring,[38] while a second contrasts Mary with Judas as alternative paradigms for disciples of Jesus.[39]

Characterization

Narrative approaches to characterization find a field ripened for the harvest in John 12. In addition to Jesus and the crowd, scholars can choose to study Mary of Bethany, the Greeks who seek out Jesus, or the voice of God. These so-called minor characters frequently have limited appearances and typically show no character development, thus appearing "flat" in the narrative. However, minor or flat as adjective descriptors for a character should not be understood to imply insignificance for their role in the plot of the narrative.[40]

While Mary has been described as a "flat" character,[41] her two appearances in John 11–12 provide distinctive aspects in her portrayal. Her position at Jesus's feet is part of her characterization, actions which reveal her as a "good"[42] or "dedicated"[43] disciple of Jesus. On the one hand, the evangelist demonstrates Mary's exemplary role as a witness to Jesus. Mary's characterization reveals itself through her actions more than by her words.[44] These actions occur at the feet of Jesus and portray another exemplary aspect of a disciple within the FG, love.[45] Given that her character represents first-century women as well, her presentation as both a witness and a disciple highlights the role(s) women portray both within the ministry of Jesus and following his ascension.[46]

Mary's extravagant outpouring provides an opulent contrast with Judas, who speaks degrading words concerning her excessiveness. A better comparison for her character might be with the unnamed "mother of Jesus" in John 2, since both demonstrate sensitivity to the timing of, as well as insights into, particular moments in Jesus's life.[47] Less flattering for her role is the characterization which has taken place throughout history that reduces Mary of Bethany's individual characteristics and conflates them with the other "Marys."[48]

The Greeks who approach Philip with their request to see Jesus represent the significance of minor/flat characters to the plot. Disagreement exists whether these individuals represent native-born Greeks who have come to Jerusalem to worship the God of the Jews, or Jews from Greek-speaking regions who have come to Jerusalem to attend the festival.[49] Their interaction with Philip recalls his initial calling to follow Jesus in 1:43–44, his role in bringing someone else to Jesus, and his verbal testimony, "We have found the one about whom Moses wrote in the Law and the Prophets, Jesus, son of Joseph from Nazareth."[50] The Greeks want to "see" Jesus, which implies in the Johannine context a willingness to believe in Jesus.[51] Another significant feature to their entry into the narrative lies in their ability, like Mary, to advance the plot and indicate the immediacy of Jesus's hour.

> The coming of the Greeks to see Jesus and their implicit intent to believe in him and his mission signals to Jesus the advent of the necessary suffering for the servant who lays down his life for a flock that breaks ethnic boundaries and encompasses the world, but also the fulfillment of his own promise for universal and eschatological salvation as the Good Shepherd of that flock, as affirmed by the voice from heaven.[52]

Although an unusual character, God the Father enters directly into the narrative when a noise is heard from heaven. One perspective sees God serving as an observer to Jesus with his vocal response signifying a recognition of Jesus. This role in recognizing Jesus "rises to the surface" when an audible sound from heaven is heard.[53] The vocal revelation of God reflects the incarnate revelation of God throughout the entire narrative.[54] When the Father responds to Jesus's request the crowd's divided response to that sound mirrors previous responses to Jesus by the "crowd."[55] This limited speech presented "on stage" serves a mimetic role in the text. Having a God who speaks "is critical to the overall purpose of the text: to have the authorial audience accept the words that Jesus, the *Logos*, speaks."[56] Those who accept the voice of God also accept the voice of Jesus.[57]

SYNCHRONIC APPROACH: RHETORICAL CRITICISM

In the previous chapter we illustrated how scholars identify ancient rhetorical practices and use those categories when examining Gospel texts. Yet, rhetoric does not limit itself solely to categories. Indeed, scholars often employ other means to discover the persuasive elements of the narrative accounts. The function of John 12 as the transition chapter between the Gospels' accounts of Jesus's public and private ministries makes it fertile for these rhetorical investigations. Other scholars seek to understand the rhetoric of the text by filtering it through social structures. The next segment describes each of these as presented in John 12.

Elements found in classical Greek or Latin rhetorical handbooks can be employed to clarify the author's rhetorical field for establishing meaning. In one instance a paradigm described by Quintilian establishes the parameters. Citing what he names the "grand style" of rhetoric, Clifton Black notes that references to the divine are significant. He describes one specific element as "calling down the gods for conversation," as Jesus does in Jn 12:28–29.[58] Jerome Neyrey also incorporates methods from classical rhetoric to examine how Jn 12:31–50 functions as conclusions for both this chapter and the first part of this Gospel. Classical authors taught their students not merely to summarize but to persuade.[59] This persuasive element, the *peroratio*, should incorporate facts or emotions.[60] Neyrey describes rejection as the rhetorical lens the evangelist establishes for his audience, "from the prologue of the narrative (1:11) to its conclusion in John 12, people have rejected the light."[61]

The examinations of historic and narrative approaches identify multiple roles for the transitional nature of John 12. When viewed through their persuasive, rhetorical role, chapters 11, 12, and 13 reveal connections that function "to help the reader perceive the continuity between these two major periods of Jesus' earthly life."[62] The emphasis on the relationship between God the Father and Jesus the Son also aids the reader in adjusting to the deceleration in story time during the account of Jesus's private ministry that follows.[63] Further clarity results when the reader recognizes the role played by the Scriptural citations in this section. Philip Harner suggests the two quotations from Isaiah transfer "the meaning of the word 'Lord' from God the Father to Jesus."[64] This transfer in referent reinforces the idea that God was active during the public ministry of Jesus. Brian Tabb sees an underlying fulfillment message within these quotations from Scripture. Not only is the prophet's message fulfilled, but God's own purpose is now fulfilled in the rejection of Jesus by "the world."[65]

Finally, social markers and social clues from the ancient world can further illuminate the persuasive elements in a text when taken into appropriate consideration. Some historical questions concerning Mary's anointing of Jesus's feet gain further clarification when one recognizes

> the feet were the body zone symbolizing action; thus, the story points to a ritual of forthcoming transformative action. Jesus is about to do something of singular significance. As [a] rather wealthy mistress of the house, Mary of Bethany takes it upon herself to acknowledge and affirm Jesus' forthcoming significant action.[66]

Social clues further highlight the summary statements found in Jn 12:31–50, where Jesus vocalizes various appeals: to join the group and to receive Jesus.[67] Customs from the ancient world demonstrate these attempts to persuade are not directed toward the characters *in* the narrative as much as they are directed toward those listening *to* the narrative.[68]

Synchronic approaches to the text often reinforce concerns expressed by diachronic ones. Structural concerns prove crucial for establishing the context for the events and dialogue reported. The existence of chapter breaks often do a disservice to the modern reader for whom the printed text disconnects John 12 from John 11 or 13. These breaks in narrative flow can also camouflage any parallel elements found earlier in the text, as in John 1, 2, or 6. A focus on minor characters in the story can provide the faceless individuals in the crowd a humanity they are often deprived of in some readings. Finally, narrative approaches seek to understand how a character contributes to the account provided in the FG instead of determining whether the character has been "borrowed" from elsewhere.

Rhetorical approaches to the text provide additional insight in response to questions surrounding the diverse elements of John 12 when compared with historical-critical questions. This renewed attention to persuasive elements in the text shifts the focus from merely learning "what can we know happened" to hearing "what the Evangelist's gospel is telling us." The modern reader can thus be moved through others' actions toward Jesus, whether positive or negative, as well as by the words of Jesus to those around him in the various scenes.

READING JOHN 12 THROUGH THEMES FROM THE PROLOGUE

Recognizing that themes introduced in the prologue get repeated in the FG is not difficult. Noting where these themes enter the discussion elsewhere in the Gospel is likewise common. The challenge this approach encounters comes in allowing these themes to color one's reading and shape one's understanding when the overriding tendency is to give preference to a preexisting historical question or even a focus on character development. In this chapter the four themes cluster in Jn 12:37–50, although RECEIVE and BELIEVE do appear in the first part of the chapter. Before assessing how these terms shape one's reading of John 12, the interceding development of the four themes in John 6 through 11 must be reviewed.

Theme Development from 6:1 to 11:57

LIFE proves prominent as a theme during Jesus's encounter with those whom he had fed across the Sea of Tiberias on the prior day. In 6:26–34 Jesus identifies life with the authentic bread from heaven, namely, the one who comes down from heaven. In 6:35–40, Jesus claims to be this bread of life, thus identifying himself as that "coming down from heaven" one. The life he describes is experienced through seeing the Son and believing. The third segment of the dialogue in 6:41–51 finds the crowd disputing Jesus's claim to be this one who originated in heaven. Jesus reinforces that life is found by believing in the Son who both came down from heaven and represents the authentic bread. The final discussion with the larger crowd in 6:52–59 connects life of the ages with resurrection at the last day and identifies this theme with the same life experienced by the Father and the Son. In a closing discussion with those still following him, Jesus reveals that life only comes through his words, that is, via the Spirit. Peter acknowledges Jesus's claim when he declares Jesus is God's Holy One, 6:60–69.[69]

Several references in John 7–10 add considerably to this image of LIFE. During the Lazarus scene, Jesus speaks with Martha and again associates himself with the resurrection. Martha often receives criticism for her limited view of both Jesus and the resurrection. Yet in Martha's confession she states her belief in Jesus as the one coming into the world, satisfying the association of Jesus with the bread from heaven in 6:26–34. She also appears to echo the understanding which associates Jesus, resurrection, and the last day found in Jn 6:52–59.

WORD, specifically Jesus's words, takes on a crucial meaning in the closing discussion of John 6. Some followers leave Jesus because the words he spoke appeared too difficult. Of those still remaining, Peter identifies Jesus's words as the source for life. In Jn 7:32–36 Jesus continues to speak words his hearers find both confusing and difficult. When he mentions returning to the Father who sent him, his audience wonders whether he is leaving to live among the Greeks. Jesus's words continue to display divisive power. When the crowd hears him offer the waters of life some profess him to be the Prophet or the Christ, while others dispute such recognition. A third group, the associates of the Jewish leaders sent to bring Jesus back to them, returns empty-handed. They can only respond that they have never heard anyone speak like Jesus.[70]

John 8 increases the division within the crowd when emphasis gets placed on Jesus's word as "my word." These words, linked here with truth, prove difficult for his audience to keep, welcome, or even hear.[71] In Jn 8:47 the evangelist identifies Jesus's words once more with those of God, words that Jesus's audience again proves unable to hear. The last segment during the Tabernacles festival closes with a renewed reminder of the division the teaching of Jesus causes.[72]

RECEIVE plays a less obvious role in this section. Philip notes that even if they spent over six months of wages, those assembled in the wilderness would only receive a small portion for food. Jesus then receives the offering of the young boy, a single day's rations, and those gathered around in groups receive however much food is needed to be filled for that moment. Later, the disciples simultaneously receive Jesus into their boat, have their fears allayed, and reach their destination.[73] During Jesus's discussion in the temple the object being received (or taken) is Jesus's own life laid down for his sheep and taken up again by him.[74]

BELIEVE is associated positively with resurrection on the last day, with receiving the Spirit, with life, and with seeing the glory of God.[75] The objects for positive belief are described as the one God sent, the Son, and the Son of Man.[76] Several statements describe positive responses to Jesus as well as negative responses.[77] Perhaps most significant are the two confessions made in Jn 9:38 by the once-blind-but-now-seeing-man associating the Son of Man with the title, Lord, and in Jn 11:27 by Martha describing Jesus as the Christ, the Son of God and the one who has come into the world.

Reading John 12:1–19 with Attention to Themes

Thomas Brodie describes Jn 11:54–12:19 as a section with two main elements.[78] The appearance of direct thematic ideas is limited; however, several actions taken by characters indicate the theme BELIEVE. By her anointing activity, Mary represents the actions of a disciple who believes Jesus unquestioningly.[79] Her faithful deeds provide testimony to the life-giving power of Jesus. Judas represents the many who fail to believe Jesus, despite being in attendance on three significant occasions: when Peter verbally affirms the life-giving words of Jesus, when Jesus shares a meal with the once-dead Lazarus, and when the extravagantly dispensed perfume infuses the private home with the aroma of life. Many Jews walk to the small town of Bethany in order to see Jesus, as well as Lazarus, and respond to their experience by believing.

The approach by Jesus to the city finds a group ready to receive their own king. Among those present in this crowd are some regaling the others with testimony concerning Jesus's action on Lazarus's behalf. Present also among the crowd are those anxious to meet Jesus. Jewish leaders, identified here only as Pharisees, stand apart from the crowd demonstrating in both word and deed their perspective on the identity(ies) assigned to Jesus in previous episodes.

Reading John 12:20–36a with Attention to Themes

In contrast to the masses who want to proclaim Jesus as king and the leaders who want to defuse the tenuous situation, a number of Greeks enter the story wanting merely to *see* Jesus, a term associated in the Johannine context with *believe*.[80] These Greeks approach Philip and Andrew, two disciples characterized previously as bringing others to Jesus.[81] This request from outsiders prompts Jesus to accelerate his discussion about his coming hour. The voice from heaven, which in its lone previous occurrence compelled JB to recognize Jesus,[82] creates division among the crowds, demonstrating that some are favorable to receiving Jesus while others remain reserved about doing so. Jesus's revelation that the time has come for him to be lifted up brings attention to the two other times this phrase appeared with regard to the Son of

Man.[83] In the first instance Jesus declares this "lifting up" as necessary before people might receive life through believing. In the second case this event brings recognition of Jesus as the "I Am" who speaks the Father's message. This third occurrence, following as it does the voice from heaven, reinforces the identity of Jesus. Light imagery at the end of the section confirms Jesus's viewpoint on his lifting up and reinforces the connection between life and the light for humanity introduced in the prologue.[84]

Reading John 12:36b–50 with Attention to Themes

In this final section of the chapter, the four themes function to amplify one another. The themes are presented in a context similar to elsewhere in John 6–11 and move from believing Jesus to receiving Jesus to finding life of the ages.

BELIEVE: John 12:37–43 seeks to explain the lack of belief on the part of so many despite the wondrous signs Jesus had wrought. The failure to believe displayed by negative responses to Jesus forms one part of the equation. Yet within this depressed forecast from the prophet Isaiah, one small ray of hope breaks through: "Despite these prophetic statements many believed in him, even from among the rulers."[85]

A diagram of Jn 12:44–45 indicates the connection between believe and see within Johannine thought.

12:44: Believe *in me* = Believe *in the one who sent me*,
12:45: See *me* = See *the one who sent me*.

This connection confirms the request by the Greeks and also recalls several other passages for reconsideration. On the first Passover trip to Jerusalem many "saw" the signs Jesus was doing and believed (2:23) while during the second Passover season the crowd "saw" signs and were following him (6:2). In Samaria the woman "saw" he was a prophet (4:19). In the bread of life discussion mentioned earlier, Jesus declares it is God's will for people to "see" the Son, to believe the Son and to have life of the ages (6:40). Even his not-so-supportive brothers encourage him to go to Jerusalem where his followers might "see" the things he was doing (7:3). Perhaps most significant, after the once-blind-but-now-seeing-man finally sees Jesus, Jesus declares his purpose as helping people see who cannot see and relates seeing him with judgment (9:39). John 12 further describes those who believe as being out of the darkness since they can now see the light, a distinct reference to John 1:5.[86]

WORD and RECEIVE: Jesus reminds the audience that his word both determines judgment and acts as judge. In addition to being an "unmistakable allusion"[87] to Deuteronomy 18:18–19, this theme recalls other statements by Jesus concerning his word and judgment.[88] These "sayings" by Jesus are described elsewhere as the words of God, as spirit and life, and as words of eternal life.[89] Those who reject Jesus by not receiving his sayings are judged by what he speaks because, like Moses and JB, Jesus speaks the Father's words since he is the Word at the Beginning.[90]

LIFE: Life and light are closely related throughout this Gospel, partly due to the connection formed between them in the prologue. Jesus declares he has "come as light into the world," recalling the comparison made in Jn 1:8 between JB who merely provides testimony concerning the light and the statement in Jn 1:9: "The true light came into the world to shine for all humanity." The references to light prepare the way for the description of eternal life as the spoken command of God which equates with those things Jesus speaks. Once again Jesus's words are associated with life, as they were in Jn 5:24, and in the summary of John 6 found earlier.[91]

CONCLUSION

Prioritizing these four highlighted themes when reading John 12 enhances the visibility of connections present within various parts of the FG. In the ancient world repetition served as one key factor in storytelling. Any repetition within the story was expected to include variation as a means for increasing the tale's value.[92] Since BELIEVE is highlighted in the anointing scene, the exemplary action by Mary demonstrates greater value than the words of Judas. The presence of Lazarus connects John 11–12 and boldly proclaims the life provided because of Jesus's trip to Bethany. Even Jesus's unorthodox entrance into Jerusalem takes on a new spectrum of color. Life and death overshadow this parade as those present at the tomb in Bethany now act as witnesses in Jerusalem. An excited and expectant crowd departs the city to greet Jesus as they would greet a returning ruler.

Life and death are present in the ensuing events ignited by the appearance of and request by some Greeks. The subsequent "truly, truly I say" statement recalls others found earlier in the Gospel. The focus on the life and death of a seed recalls the discussion in John 6, where a pair of these sayings frame Jesus's words concerning the bread of life: "the one who believes has the life of the ages and unless you eat and drink . . . you have no life in yourself."[93] The focus in Jn 8:51 further illuminates life and death: "if any keep my word they will not experience death in this age." John 10:7–10 introduces Jesus as the door for the sheep and claims, "I came so that my sheep might have life that exceeds expectations." As with John 10, the saying in 12:24–26 builds upon the initial claim in order to describe those who will follow (i.e., believe) Jesus.

The third "lifting up" explanation comes in response to divided explanations in the crowd for the noise from heaven. The emphasis Jesus places upon his own death proves perplexing to this crowd that has so recently hailed him as their king and heard this noise from heaven. They don't know whether to believe their own traditions or Jesus's words, a situation he will soon clarify.

Several scholars describe both the transitional role of John 12 and the recurrence of themes. As Lincoln notes,

> this section points ahead. Jesus will develop some of its themes yet again in his farewell discourse. And readers are prepared to reflect on the passion narrative, having been left in no doubt about the identity of the one who will experience suffering and death.[94]

Francis Moloney describes it as "a concluding summary, a gathering of the words of Jesus from across the story of his ministry."[95] Others view this narrative role as out of place or as evidence of editorial development.[96] Yet, when the conclusions identified in the previous chapter are taken into account, it becomes clear that themes introduced in the prologue reappear in close proximity to one another in at least two key moments in the plot of this Gospel, as John 5 transitions toward conflict and John 12 transitions toward death.

At the end of the last chapter, I considered John 5 through the lenses provided in the prologue and found a considerable echo with elements in Jn 1:1–11. John 12 appears to similarly echo elements in the second segment of the prologue, Jn 1:11–18. The rejection of Jesus by "his own people" (1:11) and the response by some to receive and believe Jesus (1:12) are accounted for in the words of Judas and the action of Mary of Bethany as well as in comments found at Jn 12:11, 37, and 42. JB provides testimony concerning the lofty status of this anticipated divine figure (1:15) and repeats those words (1:30) before providing another testimony concerning what he had heard from God concerning this coming figure (1:32). The crowd's response to Jesus as they welcome him to the city in Jn 12:13–15 reflects his status as one who reflects the words of the Baptizer. The glory Jesus reveals (1:14 and 18) is seen in the verbal interaction between the Father and Son in Jn 12:28. Later a stark contrast is drawn in Jn 12:43 between those seeking God's glory as revealed by Jesus and those who do not. Finally, the reference to the one who explains God (1:18) is demonstrated through the words of Jesus in 12:49–50. These similarities between the prologue and this section of the text—identified by the thematic repetition—stand as evidence for organized rather than randomly occurring composition.

Although the theme of judgment and the clouds of death hang low over the story in John 12, the light of the world still shines. Darkness is not able to extinguish this light. Instead, the light of the world shines in order that those believing will not abide in the darkness and might believe in the One who sent Jesus, who spoke from the heavens, and who is now, as he already has done, glorifying the name of Jesus and bestowing honor from God.[97] The call to believe the Word present at the beginning with God overwhelms all attempts by darkness to put out this light.

NOTES

1. Keener, *Commentary*, 2:835 and 859.
2. Bultmann, *Commentary*, ix-x. Bultmann sees a small distinction between 12:19 and 20. His displacement theory removes John 12:34–36 and 44–50 to be included in a section entitled "Jesus the Light of the World."
3. R. E. Brown, *John*, 29:427 and xii. Brown sees three subsections in John 12:1–8, 9–19, and 20–36. Brown also views chapters 11 and 12 as later additions in this Gospel's formation.
4. Schnackenburg, *St John*, 2:362–97. His units are 12:1–11, 12–19, 20–28, and 29–36.
5. Lincoln, *Saint John*, 5. Lincoln separates his discussion of John 12 into five subsections, 12:1–8, 9–11, 12–19, 20–36a, and 36b–50.
6. In addition to those comments found in longer, more comprehensive monographs mentioned previously, the brevity of this section, either 12:1–8 or 1–11, invites proposals made in shorter essays or journal articles.
7. Bultmann, *Commentary*, 6.
8. Bultmann, *Commentary*, 413.
9. Schnackenburg, *St John*, 2:366.
10. Schnackenburg, *St John*, 2:371–72.
11. Lincoln, *Saint John*, 340. Lincoln understands John to incorporate Luke 10:38–42 and 7:36–49 as well as Mark 14:3–9.
12. R. E. Brown, *John*, 29:450–52.
13. Dodd, *Interpretation*, 162–73.
14. Robert Holst, "The One Anointing of Jesus: Another Application of the Form-Critical Method," *Journal of Biblical Literature* 95, no. 3 (September 1976): 435–46, especially the conclusion on 446.
15. Keener, *Commentary*, 2:861.
16. Accounts can be found in Matthew 21:1–16, Mark 11:1–10, Luke 19:29–40, and John 12:12–15.
17. Edwin D. Freed, "The Entry into Jerusalem in the Gospel of John," *Journal of Biblical Literature* 80, no. 4 (December 1961), 329.
18. Freed, "Entry," 332.
19. Schnackenburg, *St John*, 378–79.
20. R. E. Brown, *John*, 29:471–73.
21. Schnackenburg, *St John*, 2:383–84.

22. W. C. van Unnik, "The Quotation from the Old Testament in John 12:34," *Novum Testamentum* 3, no. 3 (October 1959): 174–79. Van Unnik lists Psalm 109 (110):4, Isaiah 9:6, Ezekiel 37:25, Daniel 7:4 (LXX), as well as 1 Enoch 49:1, Psalm of Solomon 17:4, and the Sybilline Oracle 3:49–50.

23. Brian McNeil, "The Quotation at John XII 34," *Novum Testamentum* 19, no. 3 (January 1977): 22–33, and Bruce Chilton, "John xii 34 and the Targum Isaiah lii 13," *Novum Testamentum* 22, no. 2 (April 1980): 176–78.

24. Gillian Bampfylde, "More Light on John XII 34," *Journal for the Study of the New Testament* 5, no. 17 (January 1983): 87–89.

25. Talbert, "Artistry," 357–58. Talbert identifies the following similarities: Passover (6:4 and 12:1), Jesus at a meal (6:5–14 and 12:2–8), people identify Jesus as king (6:15, 26, and 12:9–19), and descriptions of Judas (6:71 and 12:4).

26. Dorothy A. Lee, "Martha and Mary: Levels of Characterization in Luke and John," in *Characters and Characterization in the Gospel of John*, ed. Christopher W. Skinner. Library of New Testament Studies 461 (London: Bloomsbury T & T Clark, 2013), 199–200. Her sections are 11:1–16 and 12:9–11, 11:17–27 and 12:1–8, 11:28–37 and 11:45–52, with 11:38–44 as the center scene.

27. Brodie, *Commentary*, 402–3. Brodie and Lincoln in endnote 5 share the same breakdown for 11:1–12:50.

28. R. Alan Culpepper, *The Gospel and Letters of John*, Interpreting Biblical Texts (Nashville, Abingdon Press, 1998), 202–3 and Keener, *Commentary*, 2:859.

29. Collen M. Conway, *Men and Women in the Fourth Gospel: Gender and Johannine Characterization*, Society of Biblical Literature Dissertation Series 167 (Atlanta: Society of Biblical Literature, 1999), 135.

30. Keener, *Commentary*, 2:859, and Sherri Brown, "The Greeks: Jesus' Hour and the Weight of the World," in *Character Studies in the Fourth Gospel: Narrative Approaches to Seventy Figures in John*, eds. Steven A. Hunt, D. Francois Tolmie, and Ruben Zimmerman, Wissenschaftliche Untersuchungen Zum Neuen Testament 314 (Tübingen: Mohr Siebeck, 2013), 398.

31. In addition to Myers, see Margareta Gruber, "Die Zumutung der Gegenseitigkeit zur johanneischen Deutung des Todes Jesu anhand einer pragmatisch-intratextuellen Lektüre der Salbungsgeschichte Joh 12,1–8," in *The Death of Jesus in the Fourth Gospel*, ed. Gilbert van Belle, Bibliotheca Ephemeridum Theologicarum Lovaniensium 200 (Leuven: Leuven University Press, 2007), 651–53 on John 2 and 656–58 on John 6.

32. Myers, *Characterizing Jesus*, 156–57.

33. Lincoln, *Truth*, 107 and 109–10.

34. For John 3, see Lincoln, *Saint John*, 353–54. For John 9, see Lincoln, *Truth*, 107. For John 10, see S. Brown, "The Greeks," 399. See Gruber, "Todes Jesu," 653–56 for John 12:1–8 and 13:1–11 as well as 658–60 for John 12:1–8 and 13:21–30.

35. David Svärd, "John 12:1–8 as a Royal Anointing Scene," in *The Gospel of John as Genre Mosaic*, ed. Kasper Bro Larsen, Studia Aarhusiana Neotestamentica 3 (Göttingen: Vandenhoeck & Ruprecht, 2015), 249–68.

36. Susan Miller, "Mary (of Bethany): The Anointer of the Suffering Messiah," in *Character Studies in the Fourth Gospel: Narrative Approaches to Seventy*

Figures in John, eds. Steven A. Hunt, D. Francois Tolmie, and Ruben Zimmerman, Wissenschaftliche Untersuchungen Zum Neuen Testament 314 (Tübingen: Mohr Siebeck, 2013), 473 and 480.

37. Miller, "Mary," 481.

38. Gruber, "Todes Jesu," 650, states "die *Einheit* von Tod und Auferstehung zum Ausdruck bringen will."

39. Gruber, "Todes Jesu," 657–58. "Die beiden Figuren sprechen nicht miteinander; jede wird unmittelbar mit Jesus in Beziehung gesetzt. Das unterstreicht die paradigmatische Funktion der beiden."

40. E. M. Forster, *Aspects of the Novel* (New York: Harcourt, Brace & World, 1927), 67–78.

41. For a description of this implication, see Lee, "Martha and Mary," 205.

42. Conway, *Men and Women*, 152.

43. Lee, "Martha and Mary," 206.

44. Lee, "Martha and Mary," 210, and Miller, "Mary," 475.

45. R. Alan Culpepper, *Anatomy of the Fourth Gospel: A Study in Literary Design* (Philadelphia: Fortress Press, 1983), 142; Lee, "Martha and Mary," 209, and Wendy E. S. North, "The Anointing in John 12.1–8: A Tale of Two Hypothesis," in *A Journey Round John: Tradition, Interpretation and Context in the Fourth Gospel*, Library of New Testament Studies 534 (London: Bloomsbury T & T Clark, 2015), 186.

46. Sandra Schneiders, "Women in the Fourth Gospel," in *The Gospel of John as Literature: An Anthology of Twentieth-Century Perspectives*, ed. Mark W.G. Stibbe, New Testament Tools and Studies 17 (Leiden: Brill, 1993), 42–43.

47. Conway, *Men and Women*, 153, and Lincoln, *Saint John*, 339.

48. Lee, "Martha and Mary," 214–15. Dorothy Lee demonstrates some Renaissance painters used a red cloak to conflate Mary's identity with Mary Magdalene. R. E. Brown notes the conflation of this account with the other anointing stories results in confusion as all three women are celebrated with a single feast day, *John*, 29:452.

49. Lincoln, *Saint John*, 348, S. Brown, "The Greeks," 400, Moloney, *Signs and Shadows*, 186–87, and Keener, *Commentary*, 2:871–72, support the native-born identification. Malina and Rohrbaugh associate these Greeks with Hellenistic Jews, *Commentary*, 211–12.

50. John 1:45.

51. Brown, "The Greeks," 401, and Moloney, *Signs and Shadows*, 187.

52. Brown, "The Greeks," 402.

53. Kasper Bro Larsen, *Recognizing the Stranger: Recognition Scenes in the Gospel of John*, Brill Interpretation Series 93 (Leiden: Brill, 2008), 182.

54. Moloney, *Signs and Shadows*, 192.

55. Keener, *Commentary*, 2:877, and Moloney, *Signs and Shadows*, 192.

56. Stan Harstine, "The Fourth Gospel's Characterization of God: A Rhetorical Perspective," in *Characters and Characterization in the Gospel of John*, ed. Christopher W. Skinner, Library of New Testament Studies 461 (London: Bloomsbury T & T Clark, 2013), 136.

57. Harstine, "Characterization of God," 139.

58. C. Clifton Black, *The Rhetoric of the Gospel: Theological Artistry in the Gospels and Acts* (Louisville: Westminster John Knox, 2013), 78–80.
59. Jerome H. Neyrey, *The Gospel of John in Cultural and Rhetorical Perspective* (Grand Rapids: Eerdmans, 2009), 333.
60. Neyrey, *Cultural and Rhetorical Perspective*, 335.
61. Neyrey, *Cultural and Rhetorical Perspective*, 337. Specifically found in John 12:31–36.
62. Philip B. Harner, *Relation Analysis of the Fourth Gospel: A Study in Reader-Response Criticism* (Lewiston, NY: Edwin Mellen Press, 1993), 23.
63. Harner, *Relation Analysis*, 25.
64. Harner, *Relation Analysis*, 11.
65. Brian J. Tabb, "Johannine Fulfillment of Scripture: Continuity and Escalation," *Bulletin for Biblical Research* 21, no. 4 (2011): 501–03.
66. Malina and Rohrbaugh, *Commentary*, 205.
67. Malina and Rohrbaugh, *Commentary*, 213 and 215.
68. Myers, *Characterizing*, 155, Lincoln, *Saint John*, 363, and Andrea Klostergaard Petersen, "Generic Docetism: From the Synoptic Narrative Gospels to the Johannine Discursive Gospel," in *The Gospel of John as Genre Mosaic*, ed. Kasper Bro Larsen, Studia Aarhusiana Neotestamentica 3 (Göttingen: Vandenhoeck & Ruprecht, 2015), 103. Emphasis added by this author.
69. Of the disciples named in John 1:37–51, only Peter is not permitted to provide a Christological title at that point. His "confession" comes in John 6.
70. John 7:37–46.
71. John 8:31, 37, and 43.
72. John 10:19–21.
73. John 6:6–21.
74. John 10:11–18.
75. John 6:40, 7:38, 11:25–26, and 11:40.
76. John 6:29, 6:40, and 9:35.
77. The positive responses are found in John 7:31, 8:30, 10:42, and 11:45. The negative responses are found in John 6:36, 6:64, 7:5, 7:48, 8:45–46, 9:18, 10:25–26, and 10:37.
78. Brodie, *Commentary*, 401. The break occurs after 12:11.
79. The prolepsis in John 11:2, her prominence as the one the Jews came to visit in 11:45 and who subsequently believed in him, and the anointing in 12:3 suggest her prominent role. Although her words to Jesus are identical with her sister's (John 11:21 and 32), she speaks them only after falling at his feet. Her voice is not heard any further in the story.
80. S. Brown, "The Greeks," 401 and Moloney, *Signs and Shadows*, 187.
81. John 1:41–42, 45–46.
82. John 1:30–34.
83. John 3:14 and 8:28.
84. John 1:5.
85. John 12:42.

86. On the complex messages being summarized at this point, see Lincoln, *Truth*, 108–9.

87. Lincoln, *Truth*, 109.

88. John 5:24 and especially the statement by Nicodemus in 7:51: "Our law does not judge a man unless it first hears from him and understands what he is attempting, does it?"

89. John 3:34 and 8:47, 6:63, and 6:68.

90. Lincoln, *Saint John*, 361.

91. See also Lincoln, *Truth*, 109, and *Saint John*, 361.

92. Talbert, "Artistry and Theology," 362. See also Stube, *Rhetorical Reading*, 79, where he cites Quintilian that through such variation in repetition "an author gives his work life and vigor and in this way is able to make the desired impression on his audience."

93. John 6:47 and 53.

94. Lincoln, *Saint John*, 362.

95. Moloney, *Signs and Shadows*, 198.

96. Schnackenburg, *St John*, 411–12.

97. John 11:28, 43.

Chapter 5

Viewing John 17 through Assorted Lenses

The four interpretive lenses we have been discussing converge once more in the discourse of Jesus with the Father before his arrest. This chapter explores this famous prayer from the perspective of diachronic and synchronic methodologies. The nature of this passage contrasts with those discussed in the two prior chapters, making the issues raised by historical, narrative, and rhetorical criticism far more diverse as well as complex. Previous analyses demonstrate frequent overlap between the methods used, especially since narrative and rhetorical criticism often utilize historical analysis as one tool in their toolboxes. The purpose for these opening comparisons is not to define any one approach; rather the goal is to illuminate the lenses through which a reader often views this chapter in the FG. Only after a reader recognizes the tendencies and limitations of the corrective lenses she or he employs can that reader begin to understand the lenses others employ. For simplification purposes in this chapter, elements from these various methods may be combined on occasion under a single aspect and noted as such.

DIACHRONIC APPROACH: HISTORICAL CRITICISM

Historical criticism seeks to answer a basic question, "What can we determine from the evidence available?" As an alternative approach it often discusses those items we cannot know for certain. When it comes to John 17, which consists entirely of monologue by Jesus, these discussions often focus on minor elements of this passage. Although comparisons with a few elements of the Synoptic Gospels are often noted, John 17 provides a unique situation for scholars to explore concepts and ideas for their veracity and probability based on the ancient world's perspectives.

Authorship

Historical-critical scholars frequently discuss what can be determined about the author of the FG. When one adds a critique of the various source elements to the scholarly mix, discussion often revolves around whether or not a section like John 17 presents an original element of the first draft of this Gospel. When Rudolf Bultmann sought to rearrange various elements to aid and assist in the "flow" of the story, at least according to his understanding of disruptive transitions, he introduced the framework for future discussions on the various drafts of this Gospel. Bultmann identifies Jn 13:1 as an introduction for the prayer found in John 17.[1] Rudolf Schnackenburg views John 15–16 as "later additions" to the evangelist's work, which makes the prayer in John 17 almost certainly a later addition as well. Even though he considers it "more probable" that John 17 was written by pupils of the evangelist or "an outstanding member of the Johannine circle," he ultimately decides it is unimportant whether a pupil or the evangelist wrote this section since the prayer "breathes the spirit of the Johannine community."[2]

In a series of published lectures, Ernst Käsemann provides an assessment of historical criticism's century-long efforts. He notes that historical criticism "fails to provide an acceptable substitute" for the author of the FG.[3] In other words, while historical critics are unable to confirm that John, the son of Zebedee, is the author—indeed they provide overwhelming evidence against such a view—they are likewise unable to provide a consensus for a replacement. Käsemann reflects a dubious opinion regarding the actual contributions of historical criticism. He notes that scholars implementing this methodology at his time in the twentieth century prefer to examine "surface problems" with this text rather than examine the "fundamental questions" the FG itself raises. These surface problems derive from "an attempt at harmonization" promoted by studies of the other three, often assumed earlier, Gospels. This type of approach may evolve into a circular argument since conclusions often merely confirm preexisting premises regarding this Gospel.[4]

John 17 as a Farewell Address

Multiple authors locate John 13–17 within the genre of farewell address used by numerous writers in the ancient world.[5] U. C. von Wahlde's analysis of the oft-named Farewell Discourse (FD) locates elements from a second and third level of authorship before concluding that the current form "is conceived of as belonging to the genre of farewell discourses, despite its complex pre-history."[6] These types of speeches were common in both Jewish and Hellenistic writings, although distinctions could be made between the "last words and testament" approach and "words of teaching and exhortation."[7] Support for framing John 17 as a prayer also finds documentation in the ancient world.[8] C. H. Dodd likens the FG's similarity to Hellenistic writings on initiation; that is to say, those in the audience rooted in Hellenistic literature would understand the FD as part of an entrance ritual into Christianity for which John 17 forms the "final stage of initiation."[9]

Structure of John 17

A natural part of analysis of the biblical text includes identifying an outline of the passage. However, simply because most scholars provide an outline for a text does not imply that they agree on how the passage should be structured. Marianus Pale Hera analyzes the structural proposals by 18 scholars for Jn 17:1–26.[10] Some see the prayer in two parts, a larger group finds three parts with the second part starting at either 17:6 or 17:9 and ending at 17:19, while fully half of the scholars view the structure as broken into four or more elements. Hera himself identifies five sections.[11] Hera's proposal falls closest to Schnackenburg's, although Schnackenburg views several verses as secondary glosses.[12] Petrus Maritz identifies two main elements, the introduction (17:1a) and the prayer (17:1b–26), with the prayer itself is divided into three subsections.[13] Edward Malatesta identifies a chiastic pattern throughout the passage with an introduction by the narrator, 1abc, with five subsequent strophes, 1def–5, 6–8, 9–19, 20–24, and 25–26. Three subsections found in 9–19 each contains a chiastic ABB'A' pattern. Malatesta considers both the structural and rhythmic patterns in identifying elements of the chapter.[14] David Alan Black describes the structure of John 17 as "more complexly organized than most discourse units in the NT."[15] His own exhaustive examination focuses on identifying the basic elements of each sentence, which results in 95 nuclear structures situated within 52 cola, that is, larger combinations of these structures.[16] Black finds the first 16 nuclear elements relatively easy to correlate (Jn 17:1abc, 1d–5), while the remainder are not so easily recognized (Jn 17:6–8, 9–19, 20–26). The structure of the unit demonstrates cohesion through its repetition of "lexical units," "syntactical structures," and "themes." The unit likewise repeats numerous elements from ancient rhetoric which work to underscore the theme of unity.[17]

These various attempts to explore the question regarding composition or authorship may come from either the diachronic or synchronic perspective. The results of such studies indicate once again the inconclusive opinions, regardless of how well each is individually argued and evidenced. Each scholar uses a set of lenses which are well adapted to the cultural era and to the philosophical perspective he or she brings to the task from prior educational pursuits. Yet, John 17 continues to provide numerous pathways of exploration, pathways previously trod by several scholars at different times.

Comparisons with the Lord's Prayer

As a result of attempts to harmonize the four canonical Gospel accounts, many compare the prayer of Jesus in John's account with the Lord's Prayer (Our Father or *Pater Noster*).[18] Raymond E. Brown identifies several shared characteristics between Matthew 6 and John 17, before identifying it as a "special prayer" and Jesus as "no ordinary suppliant."[19] Andrew Lincoln describes John 17 as "the Lord's Prayer transposed into a Johannine key."[20] Both prayers summarize what Jesus stands for, with Matthew demonstrating what the disciples should pray for while John exemplifies what "it means to pray in Jesus' name."[21] Jerome Neyrey concludes this prayer "is very different from the Our Father" and "is an extraordinary compendium of Johannine Christology."[22] Jo-Ann Brant cuts to the chase when she notes,

> Jesus violates the principles set forth in Matt. 6:7–8 regarding prayer: keep it simple because God knows what you need before you ask for it. Clearly the rhetoric of the prayer is designed not to persuade God but to lay out, before the audience of the Gospel, Jesus's concern for his disciples and how he conceives of his relationship with them.[23]

Historical-critical scholars frequently address in-depth analysis of specific ideas. Narrative critics overlap with them in this regard as they seek to identify meaning the text attempts to communicate. Three specific ideas found in John 17 receive this type of attention: the meaning of the statement in Jn 17:3 and the ideas behind God's name and behind glory.

John 17:3

The importance of Jn 17:3 in the unfolding prayer can hardly be overstated. The many discussions address questions concerning its historical status. Both Schnackenburg and von Wahlde view it as a late addition.[24] Whether the argument is framed by grammatical or thematic elements, Jn 17:3 becomes a central foundation for comments on the entire passage. Three topics dominate the interpretive comments: eternal life, knowing, and the only true God. Several factors identify eternal life as a center for emphasis. First, the emphatic demonstrative pronoun accentuates the topic introduced in the prior sentence. Second, the composition of 17:1–3 includes a series of "in order that" clauses (Greek *hina*), which draw associations and connections between sentences.[25] This type of Greek clause typically indicates purpose or result of the action described. Eternal life also appears in "a hook expression in chiastic form" that acts to join 17:2 and 3 and accentuate the description in 17:3.[26] Third, the passage recalls themes from the prologue.[27] Maritz links the idea of eternal life with becoming a child of God.[28] The introduction of Jesus's authority over all flesh in 17:2 recalls the incarnation of the word becoming flesh from 1:14. A final element, the discussion of glory, builds upon that reminiscence because in the incarnation "we beheld his unique glory."

The next element in the sentence, and one following a *hina* conjunction, is the verb *knowing*. Like *believe*, *knowing* only appears in the FG as a verb. Despite the modern tendency for information, it would appear John is not concerned with "the abstract idea" but with practical action.[29] Because knowing connects intrinsically with eternal life, understanding what "knowing" entails becomes paramount for the commentator. Bultmann associates knowing with acknowledging. Because the glory of the Father is revealed in the Son, both are part of the object of the verb. Eternal life "is nothing other than this knowledge; in it man finds his way back to his Creator, and thus has life."[30] Hera expands upon this idea and describes knowledge as "the disciples' acknowledgment or acceptance in faith of the one true God."[31] Käsemann describes such knowledge as a reference to the "truth" rather than some "anthropological and cosmological mysteries as they are communicated through apocalyptic proclamation."[32] Another concern finds expression in whether "knowing God" reflects a unique Johannine understanding or some other religious practices of the era. Craig Keener identifies several similar statements in biblical and Hellenistic Jewish traditions.[33]

While the object of the verb *knowing* is a compound—the only true God *and* the one sent—many perspectives seek to understand the phrase "the only true God" more fully since Jesus as "the one sent" appears frequently in John.[34] Von Wahlde notes similar language shared between Jn 17:3 and 1 Jn 5:20, so that his proposed third edition of this Gospel makes clear the importance of this confession of both God and Jesus whom he sent. B. F. Westcott identifies this statement as a counter to the error that results in polytheism,[35] a belief recognized far sooner, at least by Athanasius and John Chrysostom.[36] Jörg Frey recognizes the adjective "only" was applied to God in Jn 5:44, thus 17:3 reflects a cultural discussion "in the context of the religions and gods of the surrounding world" as well as in the "environment of the emergence of the Fourth Gospel."[37]

Glory

Glory and eternal life appear to be closely related. Schnackenburg notes that while eternal life does not appear again in John 17, glory replaces it as the place "in which this fulfilled eternal life is manifested."[38] Discussions of glory revolve around three primary topics: glory's relationship to Jesus in John 1–12, the OT source for the idea, and the relationship between Jn 1:14 and John 17. The FG is frequently divided into four main sections, the Prologue, the Book of Signs, the Book of Glory, and the Epilogue. Frey reminds the reader that the FD began in 13:1 with the observation that Jesus's hour was a time when the Son was glorified, 13:31–32, and was not linked to his miracles.[39] Bultmann notes that "Jesus' earthly life [that is, the Book of Signs material] was a ministry" in glory which supports Jesus's request in 17:5.[40] Furthermore, the incarnation and the glorification are inextricably linked in this hour of exaltation and humiliation.[41]

Corollaries for the word *glory* also proliferate the discussions. Hera notes glory in the FG refers to the *kavod* often experienced as the appearance of the LORD God to the OT people.[42] Frey notes "source-critical approaches scarcely bring us further with this topic."[43] Indeed, the conundrum is whether to begin in 1:14 as the "key to the whole" or in Jesus's hour as the starting point.[44] The quoted Isaiah passages spoken about in Chapter 4 from John 12 also influence the scene which is Jesus's glory.[45] Ultimately, Frey concludes, "It is God's *doxa*, which, according to the Johannine presentation, has become 'visible' in Christ, 'full of grace and truth' (1.14), i.e., for the salvation of those who 'see' him in the reading of the Gospel and in faith."[46]

The most widely discussed element of glory is the relationship between what Jesus requests in John 17 and what "we beheld" in Jn 1:14. The basic question scholars address is whether there might be a difference between these glories. Thomas Brodie depicts the movement between the glory of 17:1, "glorify your son so that your son might glorify you," to that in 17:5, "now glorify me," as a "pendulum movement" whose content "summarizes the entire incarnation."[47] He also notes these "two realities, *logos* and glory, are complementary."[48] Schnackenburg describes this glory as "the supramundane existence of the Logos, and ultimately the superiority of the divine revealer to and his transcendence over the world."[49] He further explains that this glory of Jesus is the "glory that he has possessed from eternity."[50] Bultmann identifies the glory of the Word at the beginning with God as "the revelation of God: he was God as the self-revealer."[51] This revelation was a light for men (1:5) and in the incarnation presented an alternative judgment based on acknowledging the incarnate *logos*.

God's Name

The final area drawing significant attention engages with meaning behind the name of the Father that Jesus displays to the disciples. On four occasions in John 17 the name of God is acknowledged, 17:6, 11, 12, and 25. These follow the acclaim of the crowd in Jn 12:12: "Blessed is the one who comes in the name of the Lord," and Jesus's prayer later in the same chapter, "Father, glorify your name!" (12:28). Several scholars have sought to clarify what we can know from these references to God's name.

In the ancient world, someone's name designated that person's essential identity and all that the person represented.[52] The claim that Jesus has revealed God's name indicates more than a mere announcement. Although it may only refer to revealing God, it does not mean that God was never known. Rather, as Marianne Maye Thompson notes, "the revelation of God through Jesus is *now* a revelation of God as the Father of the Son. Everything in the formulation of Jesus' identity here links him with God and points ultimately to God."[53] Yet, what is the name that Jesus has revealed?

The references to the name of God in John 17 draw heavily on OT passages which also speak about revealing God's name. Moses asks for the identity of God's name in order to confirm to the Israelites that he himself had been sent by the God of their ancestors.[54] Here the name revealed is YHWH; in Greek, *ego eimi*, the I Am. Later in the book of Isaiah, this name of God appears with reference to the forgiveness of sin.[55] Jesus claims a similar association throughout the FG.[56] The other name frequently applied to Jesus is "LORD," *kyrios*, which appears in the LXX as a designation for the tetragrammaton, YHWH.[57] The revealing of God's name and its self-referential use by Jesus further associate Jesus's identity with the Father.[58]

Whether one is seeking to use a passage's structure as the lens for reading or to compare the style of the FG with other writings, the reader finds a relatively narrow and limited scope for understanding the broader story. These types of historical-critical studies abound and older conclusions reached a century ago are frequently revisited by more recent scholarship. Unfortunately, the average modern reader of the FG does not usually have these various conclusions available to inform his or her interaction with the text. Perhaps less restricted approaches might provide a better field of view.

SYNCHRONIC APPROACH: NARRATIVE CRITICISM

Approaches to narrative criticism vary widely. Because narrative criticism examines the text in what is often called its "final form," that is to say, in the shape and form we currently possess, any methods appropriated seek to understand this version of the text. Some approaches explore characteristic use of language, while others examine the role a section may play in the unfolding plot. Smaller areas of focus are also common including the intended audience, individual characters, point of view, the employment of time variations, or genre.

Language and Plot

The multifaceted use of language in the FG has been recognized for some time. In addition to the oft-recognized double meanings of words, as in "you must be born again/from above," the evangelist employs words while changing their meaning from literal to figurative.[59] The flexibility required of a reader can be challenging to any modern reader who anticipates fixed meaning. Words like *water* and *living water*, or *bread* and *living bread*, often take on figurative meanings such as "spirit" or "flesh and blood." In John 17, studies often relate *logos* with *doxa* as well as with themes regarding the church.[60] The "interchangeability" of words throughout the Gospel must be kept in mind when interpreting John 17. Indeed, according to Maritz, the evangelist might provide readers an "interpretation key" during the account in John 2 when Jesus changes water into wine.[61]

Other scholars focus on plot development. John 17 falls at a crucial place in the Gospel since it represents the final words by Jesus in the farewell address before his arrest and ensuing death.[62] This prayer serves to restate or summarize the FD at a minimum and perhaps even the entire public ministry of Jesus.[63] As a transition point in the plot, this chapter clearly articulates the relationship between Jesus and the Father as it "highlights key concepts of Johannine Christology."[64]

Audience

Narrative methodologies often employ a focus on the implied audience as well as the actual audience of a writing. Within John 17, it is clear that Jesus speaks so that those gathered around him at this point in time are also involved.[65] The ending of John 16, "these things I have spoken to you," gives one hint to this aspect. However, the FG was not written for those disciples but rather for an external audience. Frey describes the relationship between the Gospel and its audience.

> In the Gospel of John, the story of the earthly Jesus becomes transparent for the situation of the community of addressees. This is practiced in an especially programmatic way in the Farewell Discourses. . . . Here the transparency is especially clear. The situation of the disciples' grief over the departure of Jesus "fuses" with the situation of the post-Easter community's grief over his absence, while, at the same time, the promises of Jesus, who is saying farewell, become understandable as promises for the subsequent community.[66]

The description Jesus provides in his prayer represents an ideal community, one that responds to Jesus's identity with the Father in an appropriate manner so that they can live in the love expressed between the Son and the Father.[67]

Characterization

Characterization seeks to understand ways in which a figure in the text is described. Three figures draw attention to themselves for inquiry: Jesus/the Son, God/the Father, and the disciples. In this scene, Jesus presents his identity as transparently as ever in the FG, a portrait which rivals the accounts of transfiguration found in the Synoptics. While this scene includes various rhetorical elements, which will receive attention in the next section of this chapter, here the rhetoric matches the presentation of Jesus throughout the FG. One means for determining a figure's characterization is through their language. Jesus's words represent Jesus's nature. As Clifton Black frames this, "*the grand reciprocity of John's rhetorical style*, with its ever spiraling repetition and verbal inversion, activates for the Gospel's audience the mutuality that inheres between Jesus and God, among Jesus and his 'friends.'"[68] God the Father's characterization in John 17 is fully consistent with his characterization in John 1–16, despite a change in perspective from the earlier third person to the second person in John 17.[69] The disciples, however, are not portrayed as consistently. In fact, John 17 presents the disciples in idealized language. Their earlier portrait as a group is shaped by misunderstanding or total lack of understanding, but now they seem to understand who Jesus is and fully believe in him.[70] Just as the audience appears idealized in John 17, the characterization of disciples in John 17 can be seen to represent the ideal disciple.[71] Such idealization of characters is fully consistent with this Gospel's efforts elsewhere.

> The speech of the characters in the Johannine text (with the exception of the speech of Jesus) is never identical with the message of the author. Where figures within the text (the Samaritans, the "Jews," or "the disciples") make statements, appeal to Scripture, or formulate questions and answers, these utterances must always be read as the speech of characters and distinguished from the viewpoint of the Gospel as a whole.[72]

In John 17, Jesus's words characterize the disciples in terms of how the evangelist views them, not as they may have been at the time of Jesus.

Point of View

This obvious disparity between what was and what is written can be a difficult chasm to cross. The avenue that bridges one side to the other can be found by giving attention to the point of view (POV) presented in the text.[73] The language of John 17, especially the grammatical verbal tense, can be difficult to maneuver. However, both John 15 and John 17 share a similar

POV. Jesus addresses the disciples (15) and prays aloud (17) "in the way they are *going* to be once he *has* departed."[74] This future-in-the-present perspective represents a distinct POV from the beginning of the FD. Jesus prays as though what he has said at the end of John 16 is now the reality. Thus, John 17 provides a "bridge from the fictional present into the fictional future."[75] Essentially the POV presents a divine perspective on what will be.[76]

Time

The temporal elements of the FG play an essential role in the manner by which the entire story is told. From "at the beginning" in Jn 1:1, "the next day" in Jn 1:29, "on the third day" in Jn 2:1, and throughout the Gospel, timing and temporal markers are crucial for the unveiling of this Gospel. This "looking back at what happened" is the perspective from which events are narrated.[77] The future perspective of Jesus in John 17 presents an "anachronym," in other words Jesus's language seems out of time or sync with the narrative story. The repetition of anachronyms helps draw connections between the event and its retelling. Such repetition helps build a coherent story.[78] In addition to connections made by the evangelist, the use of verbal tense also undergirds the time-distortion in the story. Grammatical expertise is not required but some awareness of grammar is. In Greek, the verbal tense structure is developed around the "active now" moment. Thus, if the evangelist emphasizes that Jesus is speaking at the same time an event is occurring, he would utilize the present tense. Most narrations take place in the present time in Greek, which is then translated into the past time for the English reader.[79] The perfect verb tense is especially frequent in John 17, implying that the narrated event has already occurred. This perspective is not merely an accident but deliberate on the part of the evangelist.[80] The result is the "constitutive relatedness of the post-Easter community to the enduringly valid word and work of Christ."[81] Such a time vortex is not limited to John 17; rather it appears at the beginning of the FD in Jn 13:31–32 and is intermeshed throughout the entire FD.[82]

Genre

The concept of genre, that is, the functional form of the text under examination, remains a key foundational item for any narrative methodology. Over the past thirty years, the FG has increasingly been associated with the ancient genre of biography or *bios*, rather than identified with the canonical Gospels as a unique genre, that is, *sui generis*.[83] Recent studies have focused on aspects of what Harold Attridge named "genre bending"—that is, the modification of typical genres for the specific purpose of the author.[84] Recognizing how genre(s) is/are adapted becomes crucial for interpreting the text in its final form. For instance, the apocalyptic genre seeks to reveal meaning through the use of symbolic language and descriptions while other genres seek to clarify and communicate meaning in their own fashion. Although the evangelist utilizes misunderstanding, irony, riddles, and other forms of micro-genres, the Gospel ultimately strives for clarity.[85]

Structural Elements

When reading through the Gospel from a narrative approach, structural elements are important. Since various outline proposals are discussed earlier in this chapter, this section will focus on the literary connections observed. Brodie provides an example. Chapter 17

> reaches behind these chapters [13 and 15], so to speak, to the texts on which they themselves are modeled, the good shepherd (10:7–18) and the prologue and it produces a structure which is a new synthesis of all these mainstream texts.[86]

One initial description of the structure includes Malatesta's charts of structure based on his analysis, which include chiastic elements as mentioned previously.[87] His charting reveals, "these themes, which appear and then vanish only to reappear, are woven together with such astonishing variety and subtle repetition and form such delicate combinations that it seems impossible to discern their precise pattern."[88]

John Boyle addresses the insight by R. E. Brown that Jn 15:11 functions as a "hinge verse" for Jn 15:7–17 and demonstrates that 15:11 is a central verse of the FD.[89] Boyle notes Jn 17:13 is likewise the "center of the whole prayer" (17:4–23) as well as the "numerical center" of the central section, 17:9–19, the prayer for the disciples.[90] Both Jn 15:11 and 17:13 focus on the theme of joy. In addition, the FD deals with the coming absence of Jesus in the first half (13:31–15:10) as does the first half of the prayer (17:4–12). Both second halves share the topic of "the hatred of the world."[91] Both elements find further connections since they "move toward union" in the first half and toward mission in their second halves.[92]

Themes in John 17

One noted commonality between John 17 and Jn 1:1–18 lies in the inclusion of similar thematic elements. While this relationship will be discussed in more detail in the closing section of this chapter, at this time some relationships should be addressed. The first step for comparing the two segments of the FG consists in identifying the various themes in John 17. Malatesta noted "no less than 44 major themes" in chapter 17 to go along with 24 themes in the prologue.[93] John O'Grady indicates sixteen themes in the prologue and remainder of the Gospel, with thirteen of those also found in John 17.[94] When it comes to focusing on different items and elements in the FG, choices do abound.

One narrative consideration lies in how a theme may impact the overall plot of the Gospel. Glory stands out as one dominant theme in John 17. Maritz suggests the verb and noun, *doxazō* and *doxa*, are used somewhat differently. As of yet, no consensus exists among scholars for a single, prominent understanding of this term. Indeed, given these distinct meanings, the question becomes how the evangelist utilizes this theme to accomplish the purpose of having witnesses recognize Jesus as Messiah and Son of God.[95] Keener notices, "a complex of associations cluster together, including Jesus' glory and love, God's name, and the revealing of God's word; this is the natural outworking of the analogy with Moses introduced in 1:14–18."[96] Glory plays a prominent role in the conflict presented in John 5, as well as in Jesus's prayer to the Father in Jn 12:27–28, affirming a certain level of plot development connected with this specific theme.

Given the development of various themes throughout the Gospel up until John 17, several words demonstrate close similarities or relationships. The two appearances by *logos* in Jn 17:13–17 suggest its significance since *logos* is connected with truth in Jn 17:17.[97] Additionally, Hera notes the close relationship between knowledge and faith.[98] Maritz proposes that glory acts as a euphemism for crucifixion in this passage.[99] These various connections provide insight but fail to find a consensus on their significance to, or meaning for, the entire Gospel.

SYNCHRONIC APPROACH: RHETORICAL CRITICISM

The discussion thus far has served to reinforce the image that the optical lens through which one views the FG affects the questions one asks and the conclusions one reaches. These optical lenses serve as paradigms for the reader of the FG since "a paradigm is the lens through which members of a discipline observe the phenomena in their areas of responsibility."[100] The traditional paradigm for two hundred years has been defined and described by historical methodology. During the past fifty years, literary and narrative paradigms have presented new ways for viewing the phenomena which is the Bible. These attempts fostered offshoots in rhetorical analysis along the lines of ancient rhetorical writings as well as utilizing numerous other approaches.

The earlier discussion of studies on the FD in light of ancient farewell addresses identified that prayer is not unexpected as a conclusion.[101] With the heightened recognition that John 17 integrates various themes of the

Gospel, Brant acknowledges "John chooses to dramatize this aspect of such a speech."[102] The question her comment raises is what element of ancient rhetoric does such dramatization reflect? As was noted in the discussion on characterization, the prayer reflects a "magnificence or grandeur."[103] The general rhetorical style is often categorized as epideictic and closely approximates a style called "leave-taking."[104] Further, this chapter's role within the FD resembles "amplification," which accentuates the grandeur of a speech and seeks to influence the audience rather than convince them of a position.[105] Recognition of such rhetorical devices illuminates the text. "The rhetorical style of the Johannine Jesus is no less revelatory than the character of the revelation that he discloses and, indeed, is."[106] Establishing rhetoric as the paradigm for viewing John 17 quietly rebukes those who dismiss certain repetitions as extraneous or editorial additions, since repetition is an essential aspect of classical Greek rhetoric.[107]

Within the FD the evangelist introduces an important new character for the ongoing Johannine traditions, the Paraclete. The Paraclete, or Spirit (Greek *pneuma*), a known commodity in the ancient philosophy of Stoicism, represents "both a material and a cognitive entity."[108] Such a paradigm leads Troels Engberg-Pedersen to compare this rhetoric with the practice in Pauline writings of *paraklēsis*. This optical lens helps describe changes in perspective in the FD, namely "the dynamic movement or change from the situation of the disciple in the fictional present, when they receive 'comfort encouragement,' to their situation in the fictional future, for which they receive 'exhortation encouragement.'"[109] This perspective on the temporal changes in the FD finds its basis in the recognition early in the FD of a rhetorical *propositio* in Jn 13:31–35. In this section Jesus first indicates he will depart and then gives them a new command.[110] Recognition of disruptions within the temporal world of the FD finds an entirely different resolution when seen through the lens of ancient rhetorical techniques as opposed to the historical lens, which views the text as having been compiled from multiple sources. The structure resulting from such an approach differs markedly as well.[111]

Genre of Prayer

Since John 17 presents itself as a prayer by Jesus spoken aloud for the disciples' hearing, it is fitting to examine its various elements through the lens of prayers in a cultural manner. Bruce Malina categorizes the types of prayer forms in John 17 to include petitionary, self-focused, and informative prayers.[112] The petitionary form represents "a request for transformation of status"[113] while the self-focused prayer is spoken in the first person and "celebrates the current role and status of the one praying."[114] The recognition of self-focused prayer can prove elusive to one who does not have that particular optical lens for viewing John 17. A prayer of this form can be "seen as a claim to the virtue of piety or justice," which represents "the noble fulfillment of one's basic duties" in the ancient world.[115] This resulting clarity presents Jesus as a virtuous client of his Patron, God the Father, a client who has fulfilled his required obligations.[116] Recognizing Jesus's example provides light on Jn 17:3, which is categorized as informative prayer. The conjoining of eternal life with knowing represents a "confessional honoring of God."[117] The disciples have now been introduced as clients of God as well and acknowledge Jesus as "the true agent sent from heaven."[118] In this schematic, knowledge is associated with two elements: acknowledgment of God as the patron and of God's plans and the honor provided to the patron.[119]

Why is the recognition of the genre of a textual passage essential? First, the scholar can focus attention on the text and what the text itself offers for interpretation rather than on issues peripherally related to the passage in question, no matter how interesting an issue might be. Second, questions about genre seek to understand the complete textual account, whether that be the FG, the FD, or merely the prayer found in John 17, rather than to pull on any dangling threads and separate the fabric of the text into unrelated elements. Third, recognizing adaptations made within a genre model serves to reinforce creativity on the part of the evangelist. Comparisons made with a standard genre pattern, much like light waves refracted through a glass prism, can reveal colorful elements which make up a combined whole. Finally, a focus on genre forces a scholar to devote more attention to what any disruptions to the pattern imply regarding the communication goals of the evangelist.[120] After paying appropriate attention to genre issues within a historically sensitive awareness, an interpreter can provide a more contemporaneously sensitive mosaic of meaning.

Theology

The third optical lens to utilize for viewing the FG lies in the theology wave spectrum. Over the past century it has been common to write on the theology of the New Testament, of Paul, or of a single writing such as the FG. These approaches examine these texts to discover how they articulate various theological principles without taking a systematic or historical approach to explaining the historical doctrines of Christianity. John 17 often becomes a focal point for these studies since, in the words of Schnackenburg, Jn 17:6–11a "contains, in a compressed form, the whole Johannine doctrine of revelation and the community of salvation, which is God's holy sphere in the world."[121] Hera suggests not only that the prayer summarizes both the FD and the FG as a whole, it also communicates "the profound relationship between Christology and discipleship."[122] Jesus describes plainly his "self-understanding of his unique relationship with the Father."[123] Thus, many Christological doctrines are derived from the FG and even John 17.

Francis Watson presents one reading of John 17 through the lens formed by the doctrine of the Trinity.[124] He highlights the "intradivine oneness of Jesus and the Father," which is opened up to allow humans "to participate in it and be one with one another."[125] He understands the unity described to be like that of the Son and the Father, but that humans also "participate in that unity."[126] While the oneness of the Father and Son is "exclusive" it also "potentially" embraces the world and humanity. For Watson, "'eternal life' is human participation in the eternal intradivine life."[127] Thus, John 17 becomes "ground zero" for discussions on the unity of the Father, Son, Spirit, and even the church. Examinations like Watson's help clarify some oft-mistaken teachings associated with the FG. Because the focus of John 17 rests on a community of Christians and not merely on some first-century male disciples, Jesus's "own" includes women as well as men, a situation clarified in the John 11–12 accounts with Mary, Martha, and Lazarus.[128] Such discussions on theology also clarify and articulate the relationship between Father and Son, which when misunderstood led to docetic understandings.[129]

Other Lenses

While numerous approaches have been applied in studies on the FG, at least three specifically view John 17 through their own distinctive lens and thus articulate a distinct—though not always conclusive—opinion. As we mentioned earlier in the diachronic section, Dodd utilized the *Hermetica* for interpreting this passage from a Hellenistic perspective. These writings demonstrate similarities with the FD and prayer by Jesus, which led Dodd to surmise that "they [the FD] are a dialogue on initiation into eternal life through the knowledge of God, ending with a prayer or hymn which is itself the final stage of initiation."[130] His attempt to unlock language which the ancient Johannine community might have automatically decoded demonstrates that the prescription lens one uses drastically alters what one can see clearly.

Two other studies deserve mention for the specialized lenses they utilize to construct building blocks for understanding the text of John 17. Jim Dekker employs a sociological construct, generativity, to examine this passage. This topic represents "the concern in establishing and guiding the next generation."[131] The world, uncertain as it is or will become, provides one concern a prior generation holds for the newer generation. Thus, the "generative person offers principles and beliefs but also tries to provide hope and support for the future, knowing the children will have to proceed on their own."[132] The introduction and inclusion of the Paraclete during the FD is simply passing the baton to a new Paraclete for the church—the Holy Spirit. Generative specialists would immediately read this as Jesus seeking "symbolic immortality." Since he is in part of the Trinity, there is nothing symbolic about this distinctly generative dynamic.[133]

Dekker concludes, "In both the final discourse and prayer we see generativity as God's modus operandi within Jesus for His disciples and those that follow after."[134]

The final study returns us back to where we began in this section on rhetorical approaches. The paradigm one selects determines one's capacity to focus on the text. Beth Sheppard suggests that Romanization might be one such useful paradigm. Since 2001, methodologies of empire have become increasingly popular over the past two decades in New Testament scholarship.[135] Here, in John 17, aspects of "absorption and local application of the forms and structures of Roman political and legal thought"[136] can be observed once brought into focus by the proper optical lens. Sheppard provides examples when Roman emperors sent heirs to the imperial throne to travel to Asia in order to express Roman authority.[137] The concept of the Roman *paterfamilias* is well documented. Thus, from this perspective

> Jesus' assertions in chapter 17 that those individuals entrusted to his care really were properly the possessions of his father accords well with the idea that God is Jesus' *paterfamilias* and that those placed under Jesus' influence and management were, essentially, Jesus' *peculium*.[138]

This Roman custom of describing father and son relationships proves helpful for explaining and clarifying some issues raised in this prayer by Jesus.

READING JOHN 17 THROUGH THEMES FROM THE PROLOGUE

Before examining how reading this prayer of Jesus "through" the prologue might appear, it may be helpful to briefly review how John 17 has been viewed as recalling various aspects of Jn 1:1–18. Three main relationships are identified: thematic, intratextual relationships, and deeper connections. As noted earlier, several scholars identify thematic connections between these two passages. Lincoln recognizes that ideas from the prologue like "pre-existence, the relation of love and unity between the Father and Son, and glory" are taken up in John 17 yet the chapter itself relates primarily to the more immediate FD.[139] O'Grady emphasizes John 17 completes the Christological emphasis begun in the prologue with the incarnation. Themes such as "the relationship between Jesus and God," "faith and rejection," "testimony to Jesus," and "light and life" found initially in the prologue present themselves in John 17. This project's attempt to read FG through lenses established by the prologue's themes is not unprecedented.

Other scholars discuss relationships between these two passages in terms of recall, whether that be total recall or vague remembrances. Wendy North links Jn 17:12 with 1:12 when she notes "the thought is wholly on the fortunes of the *tekna theou* [children of God] who are given to Jesus by the Father."[140] Others see 17:4–8 and 17:24 recalling "the beginning of John's Gospel and the Word, the Lamb of God and the Son of Man—who existed before the world was made."[141] By focusing primarily on the theme of glory, Keener finds 17:1–5 to be a "natural outworking" of the comparison of the Incarnate Word with Moses in 1:14–18.[142]

Finally, some scholars recognize even deeper relationships between the two passages. Brodie describes John 17 as a "variation on the prologue" and identifies similarities in the "essential view of history which underlies both schemas."[143] Brodie also mentions "thematic and linguistic affinities" between the two passages with examples in 17:6–8 and 1:6–7 on the use of the words "name," "sent," and "believe" as well as in 17:20–22 and 1:14 on their use of "word," "in us," and "glory."[144] Maritz draws correlations between Jn 12:27–36 and 17 in Jesus's response to the crowd.[145] Dorothy Lee describes this relationship as "an interior correlation" especially with regard to their symbolic levels.[146] The symbolic relationship "goes beyond a diachronic analysis of the Fourth Gospel."[147] In her words, "John 17 is as important as a *prolepsis* of the passion as an *analepsis* or recapitulation of the prologue in a different genre."[148]

Theme Development from 13:1 to 16:33

Themes do not exist in a vacuum; rather they are shaped by their surrounding context. While the intervening section of John 13–16 does little to advance the concept of narrative time since the events discussed in the chapter on John 12, thematic issues are enriched on the four common themes under consideration.

LIFE is relatively absent during the last evening discussion between Jesus and his followers. However, it does make two dramatic appearances. In response to Thomas's question on where Jesus is going, Jesus responds, "I am the Way, I am the Truth, I am the Life." Shortly after that, Jesus indicates, "in but a short time the world will no longer see me, however, you will see me; because I live you also will live" (Jn 14:6, 19). These two affirmations confirm life exists with Jesus and the importance of seeing Jesus, perhaps with the same sense of recognition the once-blind-but-now-seeing-man exhibits in contrast to those who do not see at the end of John 9.

WORD is crucial in John 14–15 where, in all but one instance, words Jesus spoke are recalled. At one point he responds to a question by the other disciple named Judas, not Iscariot. Judas asks how they will be able to see Jesus when the world won't. Jesus states that those who love him will keep his words—that is, his commandments. Those who don't love him won't do so. In this fashion, keeping Jesus's words parallels seeing Jesus with both resulting in life. Jesus proceeds to tell them about the coming Holy Spirit, the Paraclete or Helper, who will bring Jesus's words to their recollection. Then, bringing attention to Jesus's word to Peter during the foot washing, he indicates that his words are the cleansing agent, Jn 15:3 and 13:6–11.

Jesus's words stand equivalent to his teachings. He compares his followers' fate with his own by repeating in Jn 15:20 what he had taught them earlier at the end of the foot washing, Jn 13:16. There he describes sin as a negative response to his teaching, bringing attention to the John 9 episode again. His own prophetic word regarding the world's response to Jesus's followers becomes compared to a prophetic word from the Scriptures. Thus, the Word forges a link with the Father's commandments, which is Scripture, and responses to this concept determine one's religious standing, whether clean or unclean.

RECEIVE gains additional layers of meaning during this segment of the Gospel. The initial interplay concerns Jesus's clothing during the foot washing as he lays aside his garments before he receives/takes a towel. Once the washing is completed, he again receives/takes his garments.[149] His ensuing teaching includes the most direct statements since Jn 5:41, where again the idea of being sent underlies the discussion. The meal ensues and Judas Iscariot receives a morsel of bread from Jesus, without actually receiving the bread from heaven, Jesus himself. The Paraclete becomes the focus of receiving language in the next two appearances as Jesus clarifies that the world cannot receive God's Spirit, 14:17, and that the Spirit receives/takes from the Father and the Son to reveal to the followers, 16:14–15. Finally, the disciples are instructed to ask in Jesus's name so that they might receive and be fully filled with joy, 16:24.

BELIEVE embodies the divine name when this section opens. Jesus provides a word of teaching about a servant and his master before speaking about his own betrayer and invoking Scripture as demonstration that his word is valid. The key objective for his pronouncement is that they might believe Jesus is the I AM, 13:20, which is followed by a statement on receiving. Those still gathered after Judas Iscariot departs are encouraged to believe in God and in Jesus, 14:1, 10–12. Jesus concludes this section with another repetition, "before it happens so that when it happens you may believe."[150] Within John 16, belief is demonstrated as the opposite of sin, 16:9, and associated with loving God and receiving Jesus as one sent from God, 16:27, before the disciples confess their belief that Jesus came from God, 16:30 as compared with 13:20 and receiving the one who sent Jesus.

Reading John 17:1–8 with Attention to Themes

In this first passage all four themes appear. The first theme introduced, LIFE, is found in Jesus's authority to give eternal life to all flesh with a subsequent description of eternal life in 17:3 as knowing the only true God and his sent one Jesus. The recent identification of Jesus as "the Life" in 14:6 plays a minor role in broadening this perspective. However, since Jesus brings "eternal" life previous associations with that word likely provide greater influence on the theme.

John 17:6–8 incorporates the remaining three themes. Keeping Jesus's word was important in John 14–15 after being first introduced in Jn 8:51–55. Thus, the relationship established between loving Jesus and keeping his word, as well as the ensuing identification of Jesus as God's sent one are important characteristics.[151] These words from God spoken through Jesus are received by the disciples and form the foundation for their belief in Jesus as God's sent one. Most importantly, perhaps, is what is not included during this section—those who do not believe God sent Jesus and consequently abandoned Jesus's word.

Reading John 17:9–19 with Attention to Themes

The central section calls attention only to Jesus's word, even though a singular focus on his word is far from deficient. Jesus affirms that he has passed on God's message to the disciples in 17:14, an association clearly stated in Jn 14:24. The world responds negatively to those who receive God's message, a topic discussed in Jn 15:18–25. In the theme's second appearance God's message, which is now understood to be identical with Jesus's word, is the cleansing agent as well as truth itself. Jesus is not only life itself in Jn 14:6 but truth itself as well. The disciples' cleansing by Jesus's word is first introduced in Jn 13:1–12 and explained further in 15:3. This central section reinforces these concepts introduced since our examination of John 12.

Reading John 17:20–26 with Attention to Themes

The final verses move specifically into the generative realm discussed earlier by focusing on those who will believe because of the disciples' own message or word. On the one hand, the combination of believe in 17:20 with the prepositional phrase "through the word" recalls events at the village of Samaria, where the townsfolk initially believe in Jesus due to the woman's testimony or word. This particular phrasing links "their word" with "testifying," another key theme in the prologue. The secondary hope for the world to believe expressed in 17:21 relates to the acknowledgment and recognition that God sent Jesus. This statement by Jesus recalls his own earlier words: "Now, the Father who sent me, that one has testified concerning me. You have never heard his voice nor seen his image, nor do you have his word resting within you, because you do not trust the one he sent."[152] This prayer also repeats the request made by Jesus when standing at Lazarus's tomb.[153] Finally, attention to the relationships highlighted by these four themes accentuates the truth of Jesus as one whom God sent, and previous statements to that regard become more apparent. Three examples will suffice to demonstrate.

1. For God did not send his Son to his own to judge them, but so that his own might be delivered through the Son (Jn 3:17).
2. For the one whom God sent speaks God's words, for God gives the Spirit without limit (Jn 3:34).
3. "For the Father makes decisions regarding no one, rather he has giving all decisions to the Son, so that they might honor the Son just as they honor the Father. So, whoever does not honor the Son does not honor the Father who sent him." I speak truthfully to you, "The one who hears my word and believes the one who sent me possesses life of the ages and does not come to the judgment, rather they have passed from death into this life of the ages" (Jn 5:22–24).

Other echoes on this theme from other locations in John are too numerous to replicate here.[154]

CONCLUSION

The POV presented in John 17 places this passage in a unique position within the narrative of the FG. This POV situates Jesus—speaking in the first person—in dialogue with God the Father in the second person. The reader's position reflects that of an onlooker to this conversation between Jesus and the Father. Several items which drew attention in the earlier discussions of John 5 and 12 are absent from the prayer but present within the larger FD. The "truly, truly" sayings found in John 5 and 12 appear in John 13, 14, and 16. The first saying, which indicates that a slave is not greater than his master, 13:16, is repeated later without the "truly, truly" introduction at 15:20. The second describes receiving those Jesus sends as an equivalent action to receiving the one who sent Jesus, 13:20. Two sayings deal with failure: the betrayal of Jesus by Judas Iscariot and the subsequent denial of Jesus by Peter, 13:21 and 38. One saying discusses Jesus's followers doing the works of Jesus and greater works as well, 14:20. The two "truly, truly" sayings in John 16 look to the future and describe the joy that will follow the disciples' grief and the willingness of the Father to grant their prayers, 16:20 and 23.

Within John 17, many claims from the "truly, truly" sayings in the FD are reinforced in the prayer. Jesus declares he has finished his work, Jn 13:16, 14:20, and 15:20. We hear Jesus indicate the disciples now believe that God sent Jesus, 13:20. The reference to betrayal is repeated, 13:21. Joy finds its way into Jesus's prayer, 16:20. A final comparison returns to those whom Jesus sent, 13:20. These "truly, truly" statements function to draw attention to key ideas across both the FD and this prayer.

LIFE is clarified in the prayer. While life has been discussed throughout this Gospel, we now know that it exists in knowing, that is to say, in acknowledging, accepting, and believing God and the Word with God at the Beginning. This life is explained further throughout the prayer in other occurrences with the language of knowing. This eternal life will know what God the Father gave Jesus, which includes the word(s) of Jesus as well as the name of God, which results in love shared with Jesus and the Father, 17:7, 8, and 25–26.

WORD becomes more crucial at this stage as Jesus now speaks about a personal quality he has imparted to others, his word. Jesus explains that the disciples have kept the Father's word which Jesus gave to them, 17:6. By receiving these words, the disciples now understand that Jesus was sent by the Father, 17:8. Jesus continues to clarify that the words he has spoken/given are to result in joy for the disciples, 17:13–14. The disciples now become the bearers/speakers of this word to another generation who will believe through their testimony, 17:20.

RECEIVE finds its role within the context of Jesus's word. First, those God gave Jesus out of the world have kept his word, then they received these words, and, finally, they understand Jesus can only have come from God, 17:6 and 8. Ultimately, Jesus gives his glory to them and they, ideally, receive the glory that came from God, 17:22.

BELIEVE finds further association with knowing. Eternal life, formerly associated with believing, is now attached to knowing the only true God. Because God gave Jesus words, the disciples receive those words, know all Jesus has is from God, and believe Jesus was sent by God, 17:6–8. Because these believe, they are being sent into the world to proclaim the words they received from Jesus so that others will also believe, 17:18–20. The result of this belief is unity with the Father and the Son, 17:21.

More than in other sections within this Gospel, the interrelatedness, indeed the interdependence, of these concepts in John 17 becomes most clearly visible. BELIEVE is linked with LIFE. LIFE is coupled with knowing, which itself is tied to the theme RECEIVE. The object of receiving and knowing is the WORD Jesus himself receives from the Father. One also finds the idea of Jesus's glory becoming a central factor in all these relationships. Jesus reveals God's glory, God glorifies Jesus, and Jesus shares that glory with those who believe so that they might be unified with the Trinity, and in so doing, experience eternal life.

If any specific relationship with the prologue can be inferred from John 17, the recurring words of Jesus confirm that "the one uniquely God who was at the breast of the father, that one has explained God," Jn 1:18. In this prayer, all the revelation found in prior discourses of and signs by Jesus finds a singularly focused presentation. It might appear that everything "allocated to his ordained life and work on earth in the prologue is offered to God as completed."[155] Jesus, the Word at the Beginning, reveals God the Father. A subtle reference near the ending of the prayer, "before the foundation of the world" in Jn 17:25, recalls the opening of the prologue, specifically, "at the beginning."

NOTES

1. Bultmann, *Commentary*, 489–90.
2. See Schnackenburg, *St John*, 3:168 and 3:201–2, for his discussion on the authorship of John 17.
3. Ernst Käsemann, *The Testament of Jesus: A Study of the Gospel of John in the Light of Chapter 17*, trans. Gerhard Krodel, New Testament Library (Philadelphia: Fortress Press, 1968), 1.
4. Käsemann, *Testament*, 8.
5. Stube, *Rhetorical Reading*, 81.
6. Von Wahlde, *Gospel of John*, 2:741.
7. Schnackenburg, *St John*, 3:198. See also Käsemann, *Testament*, 4, and Lincoln, *Saint John*, 432.
8. Charles H. Talbert, *Reading John: A Literary and Theological Commentary on the Fourth Gospel and the Johannine Epistles*, rev. ed., Reading the New Testament (Macon, GA: Smyth & Helwys, 2005), 231, and Brant, *John*, 224.
9. Dodd, *Interpretation*, 422.
10. Marianus Pale Hera, *Christology and Discipleship in John 17*, Wissenschaftliche Untersuchungen Zum Neuen Testament 2. Reihe 342 (Tübingen: Mohr Siebeck, 2013), 18.
11. Hera, *Christology*, 117. The two parts are either 1–5 and 6–26 or 1–8 and 9–26. Hera's own sections consist of 1–5, 6–11a, 11b–19, 20–23, and 24–26.
12. Schnackenburg, *St John*, 168–69.
13. Petrus Maritz, "The Glorious and Horrific Death of Jesus in John 17: Repetition and Variation of Imagery Related to John's Portrayal of the Crucifixion," in *The Death of Jesus in the Fourth Gospel*, ed. Gilbert van Belle, Bibliotheca Ephemeridum Theologicarum Lovaniensium 200 (Leuven, Belgium: Leuven University Press, 2007), 704.

14. Edward Malatesta, "The Literary Structure of John 17," *Biblica* 52, no. 2 (1971): 210–11.

15. David Alan Black, "On the Style and Significance of John 17," *Criswell Theological Review* 3 (Fall 1988): 145–47. Malatesta and D. A. Black represent synchronic approaches.

16. For example, John 17:1 is broken into six nuclear structures: (1) Jesus spoke these things, (2) and lifted his eyes toward the heavens, (3) he said, (4) Father, the hour has come, (5) Glorify your Son, (6) so that he might glorify you. Black does not identify the cola in his analysis.

17. Black, "John 17," 145, 148–54.

18. William O. Walker, Jr. "The Lord's Prayer in Matthew and John," *New Testament Studies* 28, no. 2 (April 1982): 237–56.

19. R. E. Brown, *John* 29A:747–48.

20. Lincoln, *Saint John*, 433.

21. Lincoln, *Saint John*, 433.

22. Jerome H. Neyrey, *The Gospel of John*, New Cambridge Bible Commentary (Cambridge: Cambridge University Press, 2007), 287–88. Neyrey finds closer parallels with the Our Father prayer in Jesus's prayer reported in John 12:27–28. Neyrey and Brant represent synchronic approaches.

23. Brant, *John*, 224.

24. Schnackenburg, *St John*, 3:172, and von Wahlde, *Gospel of John*, 2:716–17. Von Wahlde identifies this as the only mention of "eternal life" in the third edition.

25. Hera, *Christology*, 129. See Keener, *Commentary*, 2:1055, for an argument about not making too much of the grammatical construction from a Greek perspective.

26. Malatesta, "Literary Structure," 197.

27. Lincoln, *St John*, 432.

28. Maritz, "Death," 706, as in John 1:12.

29. Westcott, *St. John*, 239.

30. Bultmann, *Commentary*, 494–95.

31. Hera, *Christology*, 130.

32. Käsemann, *Testament*, 6.

33. Keener, *Commentary*, 2:1054. See also Lincoln, *Saint John*, 435, and Schnackenburg, *St. John*, 172.

34. John 3:17, 34; 5:36–38; 6:39, 57; 7:29; 8:42; and 11:42.

35. Brooke Foss Westcott, *The Gospel According to St. John* (London: John Murray, 1896), 239.

36. Athanasius, *Orations against the Arians*, 3.23.6–24.8–9, and John Chrysostom, *Homiliae in Joannem*, 80.2. See Schnackenburg for other comments by early writers, *St John*, 3.173.

37. Jörg Frey, *The Glory of the Crucified One: Christology and Theology in the Gospel of John*, trans. Wayne Coppins and Christoph Heilig, Baylor-Mohr Siebeck Studies in Early Christianity (Waco: Baylor University Press, 2018), 319.

38. Schnackenburg, *St John*, 3:172.

39. Frey, *Glory*, 250.

40. Bultmann, *Commentary*, 493.
41. Bultmann, *Commentary*, 493.
42. Hera, *Christology*, 45.
43. Frey, *Glory*, 239.
44. Frey, *Glory*, 241.
45. Frey, *Glory*, 245–46.
46. Frey, *Glory*, 258. In doing so he confirms Hera's association with *kavod*.
47. Brodie, *Commentary*, 511.
48. Brodie, *Commentary*, 516.
49. Schnackenburg, *St John*, 3:174.
50. Schnackenburg, *St John*, 3:195.
51. Bultmann, *Commentary*, 496.
52. Lincoln, *Saint John*, 435–36, and Keener, *Commentary*, 2:1056.
53. Marianne Meye Thompson, *John: A Commentary*, New Testament Library (Louisville: Westminster John Knox, 2015), 351.
54. Exodus 3:13.
55. Von Wahlde, *Gospel of John*, 2:724, 731.
56. Lincoln, *Saint John*, 436.
57. Thompson, *John*, 352–53.
58. Von Wahlde, *Gospel of John*, 3:731.
59. Maritz, "Death," 695.
60. Maritz, "Death," 704.
61. Maritz, "Death," 709.
62. Keener, *Commentary*, 2:1050, and Black, "John 17," 154.
63. Lincoln, *Saint John*, 440. See also Hera, *Christology*, 15–18.
64. Hera, *Christology*, 90, Black, "John 17," 154.
65. Black, "John 17," 144.
66. Frey, *Glory*, 90. See also Jo-Ann Brant in the discussion on the Lord's Prayer at n. 23.
67. Hera, *Christology*, 168.
68. C. Clifton Black, "'The Words That You Gave to Me I Have Given to Them': The Grandeur of Johannine Rhetoric," in *Exploring the Gospel of John: In Honor of D. Moody Smith*, eds. R. Alan Culpepper and C. Clifton Black (Louisville: Westminster John Knox Press, 1996), 228–29.
69. Harstine, "Characterization of God," 144.
70. Hera, *Christology*, 142 and 167.
71. Hera, *Christology*, 143.
72. Frey, *Glory*, 93.
73. For a perspective on point of view in the entire Gospel, see James L. Resseguie, "Point of View," in *How John Works: Storytelling in the Fourth Gospel*, eds. Douglas Estes and Ruth Sheridan (Atlanta: SBL Press, 2017), 79–96.
74. Troels Engberg-Pedersen, "A Question of Genre: John 13–17 as Paraklēsis," in *The Gospel of John as Genre Mosaic*, ed. Kasper Bro Larsen, Studia Aarhusiana Neotestamentica 3 (Göttingen: Vandenhoeck & Ruprecht, 2015), 294.
75. Engberg-Pedersen, "Genre," 296.

76. See Westcott, *St. John*, 237, for a similar description although his approach preceded the formalized narrative methods by a century.

77. For a perspective on time in the entire Gospel, see Douglas Estes, "Time," in *How John Works: Storytelling in the Fourth Gospel*, eds. Douglas Estes and Ruth Sheridan (Atlanta: SBL Press, 2017), 41–57. See also Frey, *Glory*, 85.

78. Estes, "Time," 52.

79. For example, the Greek word *legō*, I say or speak, appears in the present tense 221 times in the FG. It appears 259 times total in every other tense. "He says" appears 127 times in the present tense and 130 times total in every other tense.

80. Frey, *Glory*, 79–80.

81. Frey, *Glory*, 81–82.

82. Frey, *Glory*, 89.

83. For a discussion of genre, see Harold W. Attridge, "Genre," in *How John Works: Storytelling in the Fourth Gospel*, eds. Douglas Estes and Ruth Sheridan (Atlanta: SBL Press, 2017), 7–22. For a discussion of the genre of *bios* and the FG, see Harstine, *Moses*, 16.

84. Harold W. Attridge, "Genre Bending in the Fourth Gospel," *Journal of Biblical Literature* 121, no. 1 (Spring 2002): 3–21.

85. Engberg-Pedersen, "Genre," 285.

86. Brodie, *Commentary*, 506.

87. Malatesta, "Literary Structure." His section III, Jn 17:9–19, demonstrates a dominant aba´ pattern with the center section, vv. 11d–16, exhibiting an abb´a´ pattern. Panel B indicates these elements as a (11d–g) b (12), b´ (13–14) and a´ (15–16). Section IV exhibits an abcb´a´ parallel structure with the center emphases in v. 22a–c.

88. Malatesta, "Literary Structure," 190–91.

89. John L. Boyle, "The Last Discourse (Jn 13, 31–16, 33) and Prayer (Jn 17): Some Observations on Their Unity and Development," *Biblica* 56, no. 2 (1975): 216 where he is quoting R. E. Brown, *John* 29A:667.

90. Boyle, "Last Discourse," 220.

91. Boyle, "Last Discourse," 220–21.

92. Boyle, "Last Discourse," 222.

93. Malatesta, "Literary Structure," 190n2.

94. John F. O'Grady, "The Prologue and Chapter 17 of the Gospel of John," in *What We Have Heard from the Beginning: The Past, Present, and Future of Johannine Studies*, ed. Tom Thatcher (Waco: Baylor University Press, 2007), 218.

95. Maritz, "Death," 697–98. John 20:31.

96. Keener, *Commentary*, 2:1052.

97. Hera, *Christology*, 153.

98. Hera, *Christology*, 174–75. See also Brodie, *Commentary*, 512.

99. Maritz, "Death," 709.

100. Martha Hale, "Paradigmatic Shift in Library and Information Science," in *Library and Information Science Research: Perspectives and Strategies for Improvement*, eds. C. R. McClure and P. Herndon (Norwood, NJ: Ablex Publishing Corp, 1991), 343, quoted in Beth M. Sheppard, "The Rise of Rome: The Emergence of a New Mode for Exploring the Fourth Gospel," *ATLA Summary of Proceedings* 57 (2003): 175.

101. Stube, *Rhetorical Reading*, 188.
102. Brant, *John*, 224.
103. Black, "Grandeur," 221, compares this to Demetrius's writing *On Style* who calls this style "*to megaloprepes*."
104. Black, "Grandeur," 224, *suntaktikos*.
105. Black, "Grandeur," 224–25, *auxesis*. See Stube, *Rhetorical Reading*, 78, for further discussion of rhetorical amplification.
106. Black, "Grandeur," 229.
107. Stube, *Rhetorical Reading*, 211–12.
108. Engberg-Pedersen, "Genre," 298.
109. Engberg-Pedersen, "Genre," 298.
110. Engberg-Pedersen, "Genre," 290.
111. Engberg-Pedersen, "Genre," 295–96. Engberg-Pederson identifies an ABA'B' structure consisting of 13:31–14:31, 15:1–16:15, 16:16–33, and 17:1–26.
112. Bruce J. Malina, "What Is Prayer?" *The Bible Today* 18 (July 1980): 214–20, as cited in Neyrey, *John*, 276–81.
113. Neyrey, *John*, 279.
114. Neyrey, *John*, 280.
115. Neyrey, *Cultural and Rhetorical Perspective*, 391.
116. Neyrey, *Cultural and Rhetorical Perspective*, 392–93. See also Malina and Rohrbaugh, *Commentary*, 244, and Käsemann, *Testament*, 11, who uses the term "delegate" who was attested in rabbinic writings as "equal to the sender."
117. Neyrey, *Cultural and Rhetorical Perspective*, 392.
118. Neyrey, *Cultural and Rhetorical Perspective*, 393.
119. Neyrey, *Cultural and Rhetorical Perspective*, 393.
120. Engberg-Pedersen, "Genre," 282.
121. Schnackenburg, *John*, 3:175.
122. Hera, *Christology*, 90.
123. Hera, *Christology*, 90.
124. Francis Watson, "Trinity and Community: A Reading of John 17," *International Journal of Systematic Theology* 1, no. 2 (July 1999): 168–84.
125. Watson, "Trinity and Community," 170.
126. Watson, "Trinity and Community," 170.
127. Watson, "Trinity and Community," 171.
128. Watson, "Trinity and Community," 173.
129. Watson, "Trinity and Community," 175–80.
130. Dodd, *Interpretation*, 420–22.
131. Erik H. Erikson, *Childhood and Society*, 2nd ed. (New York: Norton, 1963), 267, as quoted in Jim Dekker, "Generativity, Covenant Witness, and Jesus' Final Discourse," *Ex Auditu* 28 (2012): 148.
132. Dekker, "Generativity," 152.
133. Dekker, "Generativity," 153.
134. Dekker, "Generativity," 155.
135. See Gregory Riley, *The River of God* (San Francisco: HarperCollins, 2001).

136. Clifford Ando, *Imperial Ideology and Provincial Loyalty in the Roman Empire* (Berkeley: University of California Press, 2000), xi, quoted in Sheppard, "Rise of Rome," 178.

137. Sheppard, "Rise of Rome," 179.

138. Sheppard, "Rise of Rome," 180. The Roman *peculium* was property over which the recognized adult heir would have "almost complete administrative freedom" despite not yet owning the property.

139. Lincoln, *Saint John*, 432.

140. Wendy E. S. North, "'The Scripture' in John 17.12," in *A Journey Round John: Tradition, Interpretation and Context in the Fourth Gospel*, Library of New Testament Studies 534 (London: Bloomsbury T & T Clark, 2015), 49.

141. Malina and Rohrbaugh, *Commentary*, 244–45.

142. Keener, *Commentary*, 2:1052. See also Maritz, "Death," 699, who sees 1:14 as "one of the pivotal steering points in the Gospel" with regard to the theme of glory.

143. Brodie, *Commentary*, 508–9.

144. Brodie, *Commentary*, 510.

145. Maritz, "Death," 702.

146. Dorothy Lee, "The Prologue and Jesus' Final Prayer," in *What We Have Heard from the Beginning: The Past, Present, and Future of Johannine Studies*, ed. Tom Thatcher (Waco: Baylor University Press, 2007), 230.

147. Lee, "Prologue," 231.

148. Lee, "Prologue," 231.

149. This is a similar situation as Jesus's statement in 10:17–18 regarding taking and receiving.

150. John 14:29 repeats 13:19.

151. Stube, *Rhetorical Reading*, 209.

152. John 5:37–38.

153. The only difference is a change in the verb tense from "they might believe" to "they believed" that you sent me, John 11:42.

154. See John 5:36–38, 6:29, 6:57, 8:16–18, 14:24 to cite a few instances.

155. Harris, *Prologue and Gospel*, 194.

Chapter 6

Closing Observations

The approach in this monograph has been to compare and highlight the results obtained when using various methods for studying the Gospel of John. On the highest level, these methods distinguish themselves from each other by the way they perceive the Gospel using chronological time. Traditional methodologies such as historical criticism, source criticism, form criticism, or redaction criticism assume the FG represents a text developed in multiple stages over time. A compositional history of this type requires a series of accounts about the life of Jesus written sometime during those years following Jesus's death until the Gospel obtained its most recent form. This developmental approach is identified by the term *diachronic*, literally "through-time." Over the past fifty years scholars started to employ other types of methodologies as they began to find the results from these diachronic methods less than satisfactory or conclusive. These newer approaches seek to understand varying elements of the Gospel as it exists in its most recent state, often called its "final form." This perspective on the FG is often termed *synchronic*, literally "with-time." These two distinct approaches often reach quite distinct conclusions. More importantly, a reader should recognize that these distinct conclusions arise from distinct questions that scholars ask. For the reader of the FG, the questions one seeks to understand determine the trajectory of the inquiry.

On a more practical level, this book provides a comparative perspective on historical, narrative, and rhetorical approaches to four passages in this Gospel: Jn 1:1–18 and chapters 5, 12, and 17. The analogy of an optical lens, which can come in different levels of magnification and correction in order to help a person see more clearly, has been employed to describe these diverse comparisons. A reader who employs a historical methodology rather than a narrative method would be like someone who wears eyeglasses that correct deficiencies for distance vision rather than a pair for reading. Another illustration would be choosing to wear polarized sunglasses instead of non-polarized ones. Either corrective lens will affect the clarity of the user when looking at the same element. Yet, more than merely presenting a survey of approaches by other scholars to the Gospel of John, this volume incorporates a further approach, one which examines how the prologue itself provides clarity for examining the FG. This method assumes the Fourth Evangelist developed a specific manner for speaking, later captured in written form, which utilized key words or *Leitwörter* as a means for communicating important principles. The four key themes discussed appear frequently throughout the FG because they communicate the key ideas of this evangelist. The insights discussed in chapters 3–5 argue strongly for the benefit this approach provides a reader. The final decision on whether to invest in a new set of prescription lenses ultimately rests in the eyes of the beholder.

The first stage in this concluding chapter will review the results from the previous chapters. Were any new results brought to light on these four selected themes by focusing on them throughout these selected passages? Did LIFE, WORD, RECEIVE, or BELIEVE gain additional depth or breadth of meaning? The large scope of this venture permits only a collation of the details highlighted. A second stage provides an analysis comparing these insights with those determined through the other methods. Finally, after completing these steps I will suggest some probable conclusions regarding the unity of the Gospel of John.

REVIEW OF THE FOUR THEMES

Chapter 1 establishes the importance of the prologue to the FG and identifies the most likely themes for this study. Chapter 2 provides an example of how a detailed focus on two themes can reveal additional insight, meaning, or emphasis. Chapters 3, 4, and 5 engage in the heavy lifting necessary for sifting through the mountains of data. What then did we unearth with regard to the themes we mined?

Life

Chapter 3 acknowledges that life originates in the *Logos* and is associated with the Son of Man lifted up. Such life is recognized as eternal life or life of the ages. When Jesus heals the man in John 5, he makes him "whole," a term which acts as a synonym for this eternal life. Jesus's actions mirror the Father's deeds and are described as life-giving. These life-giving actions are associated with Scripture, more specifically with believing Scripture and believing Jesus's word. Chapter 4 associates this theme with Jesus the bread of life descended from heaven. Life of the ages is described as that which the Father and Son share. Furthermore, this life is available through Jesus's word. Believing Jesus's word becomes crucial for obtaining this type of life. The life provided is the light of the world and exists as the words of God which Jesus speaks. In chapter 5 we find this life is Jesus, or more precisely, Jesus is the Life. Those who actually "see" Jesus experience this life. Jesus provides this life of the ages, a life specifically associated with knowing God and Jesus. This life comes through Jesus's words because the Father gave them to Jesus who is the Word at the Beginning.

Word

In chapter 3, a monologue by Jesus serves to establish the central point. Jesus's words function as both the center of the contention and the means for communicating his identity. This imagery builds upon the recognition that Jesus's words are memorable and require believing. In John 5 the words of Jesus bring healing to the man who cannot move into the water without help from others. The man receives and believes Jesus's spoken word to him. Three "truly, truly" sayings emphasize the word of Jesus, with the last two connecting his word with life-giving power. Finally, since Jesus's words find close association with God's own words and with Moses's writings the question is raised whether Jesus's words will be believed.

Chapter 4 indicates further development of this theme after John 5. Peter associates Jesus's words with life. Jesus's words are increasingly seen to create division between those who receive them and those who do not. His words are reaffirmed as those of God. Finally, Jesus speaks life-giving words at Lazarus's tomb. John 12 strengthens the concept that Jesus's words are decisive and recalls words by Moses in Deuteronomy 18, reinforcing the idea that judgment accompanies such division. When one believes the words of Jesus, one is believing the words the Father gave him.

Chapter 5 recalls the words of Jesus during his last evening with the disciples, words the Paraclete will help them recall later. Keeping these words, also described as receiving and believing them, becomes a major emphasis. In the prayer of John 17, Jesus's words take center stage. Jesus has passed on the Father's words and the world has been divided over them. These words are life and truth just as Jesus is Life and Truth. These words are to be kept, resulting in great joy, and shared with others so that they too might believe in Jesus.

Receive

Chapter 3 demonstrates the adverse side of failing to receive the Word at the Beginning. Not everyone will receive Jesus's testimony; one can only receive what one has been given from heaven. In John 5 the temple leaders do not receive three distinct items: all the words from the healed man, the sign which is his healing, and what Jesus has to say. Jesus's monologue at the end establishes the perspective that many will fail to receive his words.

Chapter 4 identifies contrasting viewpoints toward receiving. In Philip's view the crowd will only receive a small portion of the meal, but the heavenly blessing provides as much as they need. The disciples receive Jesus into their boat in the midst of the Sea of Galilee, yet immediately arrive at their target destination. Finally, one major question centers on receiving Jesus's own life laid down for others. In John 12 the crowd cheers as they receive their king, yet he is not a king who will lead them in their fight against Roman rule. The now third occurrence of the statement that Jesus must be "lifted up" results in a crowd divided over whether they should receive this notice or not. The act of receiving Jesus's words represents a crucial step in the judgment decision. Those who receive these words, which are the Father's words, receive no condemnation.

Chapter 5 reveals the layers of meaning this theme contains in itself. Jesus lays down his garments and takes them up again. The Paraclete must also be received, yet not everyone can receive God's Spirit. John 17 identifies the focus must be on receiving the words spoken by Jesus, words which originate with the Father. A series of stages in this process appear to be present. One must receive the words of Jesus in order to understand his identity; then one can receive the glory that only comes from God.

Believe

Chapter 3 demonstrates the dominant role BELIEVE plays in the plot of this Gospel. One is to believe in the name given, one is to believe Scripture and the word of Jesus, one cannot believe unless one first receives Jesus's teaching. In John 5, discussions around this theme adopt a dominant posture toward the failure to believe. This scene characterizes the other group as not believing God, Moses, or Jesus. The failure by these leaders to receive the man's healing provides a link with the ensuing judgment.

Chapter 4 expands the semantic domain to include resurrection and emphasizes positive responses as well as negative ones. Believing results in confession and greater recognition of Jesus's identity. John 12 provides contrasting responses by those believing or failing to do so. Not everyone in Jerusalem believes even though they see Jesus in the city. The themes seeing and believing coalesce in the request by some Greeks. Although strongly colored by the failure by many to believe, in agreement with the prophet Isaiah some do believe in Jesus.

Chapter 5 portrays the positive aspect of believing, especially Jesus's true identity. One will ultimately believe Jesus to be the I Am. John 17 clarifies that a person must believe God sent Jesus. Only then can someone believe the words of Jesus are the words of God. Those who believe this basic aspect are also sent as Jesus was sent. The final result of believing is unity with God the Father and Jesus the Son.

Testimony

Chapter 3 demonstrates that other themes from the prologue may also be relevant for a discussion on repetition, even when they don't appear in every location. We find in the opening chapters of the Gospel an emphasis on others testifying (verb) or sharing testimony (noun) about what they have learned of Jesus. John the Baptizer declared that he was *not* the eschatological figure they expected but that this figure was among them even as he was speaking. The healed man tells the Jerusalem religious leaders a man healed him, an eschatological act, yet they were more interested in a violation of Torah than in his testimony. In Jesus's monologue, JB's earlier testimony pales in comparison to the testimony of another witness, God the Father. The failure on the part of many to receive the lesser testimony prevents them from accepting any testimony, no matter how great or persuasive. Chapter 5 infers the giving of testimony from earlier in the Gospel by providing verbal clues to what happened in the village of Samaria and to words by JB. Jesus's followers will now be the ones providing testimony as they are sent into the world.

ANALYSIS

These four themes can be, and indeed often are, read as separate and unrelated aspects of this Gospel. However, when allowed to shape the lens through which one reads the FG, by the time the reader reaches the end of John 17 these four themes stand not as separate individual pillars but rather as interlocking timbers forming the walls of a building. Although the prologue initially appears to introduce these themes as separate and distinct concepts and although John 5 might at first appear to continue this more nuanced presentation, the themes intertwine more tightly as the Gospel plot unfolds. John 12 utilizes seeing as an analogy for believing while John 17 employs the analogy of knowing. The reader of the FG is to receive and believe the word of Jesus. Meanwhile, the word of Jesus serves as the point of division between those who will and those who will not receive and believe. Those who do receive and believe these words experience the life of the ages made available to them and those who won't, don't.

Although the close proximity of these four themes draws attention to John 5, 12, and 17, the meaning these themes develop is not limited only to these passages. The healing of the man born blind in John 9 establishes the concept of seeing as an analogy for believing.[1] The relationship between knowing and believing appears as early as Jn 4:53 when the father acknowledged his son was healed at the same hour as Jesus's announcement. The confession by Peter at Jn 6:69 draws this connection between the two themes even tighter. Their association intensifies at Jn 7:16 and during the ensuing conversation in 8:31–54. The attentive reader slowly begins to recognize the interconnection between these themes throughout the FG as these individual threads are woven more tightly together.

Furthermore, analysis of the plot of the FG indicates these themes congregate at significant transition points in the Gospel. In John 5 the plot introduces the increasing conflict with religious leaders in Jerusalem, while John 12 transitions from Jesus's public ministry among the crowds to his withdrawn ministry among his followers. John 17 represents a transition from Jesus's life to his death, from his time to his hour, from his incarnate form to his ascended glory. Thematically, the plot moves from Jesus's own testimony about himself to God's testimony on his behalf, from the glory men seek to bestow on each other to the revealed glory the Father has bestowed on the only Son.

UNITY OF THE GOSPEL

Chapter 1 described the characteristic diachronic recognition of disruptions in the text as evidence for a lack of unity. Scholarly attempts to counter such conclusions utilizing the same diachronic methodology frequently serve merely to demonstrate the overwhelming influence of both sides' starting assumptions.[2] Narrative approaches typically set aside such conclusions at the onset of study for the sake of working with a complete text. Yet, due to the diverse elements of narrative methods these studies often separate the story into disparate pieces such as plot, character, or genre. What does the approach of this book based on themes introduced in Jn 1:1–18 indicate with regard to these challenges?

The thematic approach taken in this volume contains its own set of assumptions. One such presumption acknowledges that if the FG is a unified work, then that unity is based on a singular author—whether that person be the Fourth Evangelist or a successive editor. Consequently, the author of the prologue functions as the party responsible for the close proximity of these themes at Jn 5:31–47, 12:36b–50, and 17:1–8. Any subsequent investigation into the FG's unity would require detailed analysis of conclusions scholars using diachronic methods draw regarding these passages.

For example, Urban C. von Wahlde indicates Jn 5:31–47 belongs to the second edition of the Gospel's composition, 12:36b–50 contains elements from all three editions,[3] and 17:1–8 contains additions from the second and third editions.[4] In John 12, the passage from the first edition incorporates the theme of believing, although presented in the negative as the failure to believe. The quotation from Isaiah and the narrator's comment that many of the leaders were believing in him belong to a third edition passage. All four themes appear in the second passage that von Wahlde assigns to the third edition, 12:46–50. In von Wahlde's reconstruction these themes appear across his three editions.[5]

A second approach for determining unity would follow the line of thought, "what proposal best describes the concentration of these themes in these three passages?" Three questions further illuminate the positive and negative aspects of the predicament.

1. Do the themes already exist in an earlier version of the Gospel so that the prologue is composed at a later time to draw attention to these passages?
2. Does the author of the prologue edit earlier material by adding these passages at key transition points to enhance a particular way to read the Gospel?
3. Does the presence in these three transitional passages of these four significant themes from the prologue indicate a greater unity than diachronic approaches have proposed?

Synchronic examinations of elements of the Gospel provide highly plausible and culturally appropriate responses to issues raised by diachronic methods regarding disruptions and repetitions in the FG. From their modern viewpoint Bultmann and others found the Farewell Discourse too full of disruptions to be viewed as a unified section. Scholars have now demonstrated that the FD follows a pattern of parallel construction consistent with ancient practices. The prayer in John 17 can now be viewed as a concentric rather than linear way of thinking. Challenges to Jesus's discourse in John 5 often find their basis in presuppositions found in the quest for the historical Jesus. This filter typically dismisses them as words of the actual Jesus and instead views them as a disruption to some "earlier" written version of the Gospel account. Studies on John 5 identify chiastic relationships with preceding and subsequent passages, thus sealing this oft cited fissure. Findings from the social sciences on ancient practices of patron and client relationships demonstrate that Jesus acts as God's agent in both John 5 and John 17.

A focus on rhetorical practices common to the era suggests the FG incorporates elements of Greco-Roman rhetoric within the speeches/discourses by Jesus. Such approaches illuminate Jesus's words as persuasive language for the audience of the Gospel, not necessarily the audience addressed by Jesus's monologue. Speeches by Jesus found in John 5, 12, and 17 each fall into this category. The words recorded are better understood when not viewed as mere recitation of shared information and when not judged against the synoptic materials.

Granting attention to techniques used by ancient practitioners for oral and written presentations causes those disruptions within the text observed by modern readers to be seen as far less problematic than they have been previously described. Continuing to examine a text under the same optical lens will magnify those elements identically, regardless of who utilizes that lens. Rather than attempt to identify and correct every viewpoint on the Gospel of John, the approach taken in this monograph demonstrates the lenses one uses for studying a text will impact how that reader understands certain elements in the text. It is this author's hope that this thematic approach will challenge any reader of the FG to use several different lenses before drawing any firm conclusions. Ultimately, these chapters have shown that a pair of standard, over-the-counter eyeglasses may not be the best available option for observing the beauty within the FG.

FINAL PROPOSITIONS

What, then, is the probability that the Gospel of John represents a unified text in its current form and shape? I have indicated elsewhere the propensity by biblical scholars to question the unity of the prologue with the result that no one approach could ever answer all the difficulties raised.[6] Based on the evidence accumulated in this present approach, which I have elsewhere referred to as the "helical" reading,[7] I would offer the following three propositions for further consideration.

1. The convergence of themes at these transitional passages is not accidental. The evangelist intentionally brings them together to catch the attention of the ancient listener and reader.
2. Modern approaches, which seek to define a word and limit its meaning to that pre-assigned definition, do not recognize the fluidity of language, whether modern or ancient. Words gain meaning through their use within a specific context. While some common meaning continues to be involved in the communication process a word's connotation in the present context is not limited by its use elsewhere in a different context.
3. The replacement of certain words with euphemisms, synonyms, lexical domain similarities, or analogies requires further study. Just as scholarship has shown no differences in the Johannine text between the words

phileō and *agapaō*, it is likely the Fourth Evangelist utilizes other word sets for stylistic reasons.

Given the evidence currently available I find it most probable that these key themes developed within the oral tradition of the Fourth Evangelist. Their repeated appearances with an increasing level of complexity and the attraction of these themes at key points in the plot of the FG are due to a single authorial voice. In the movie *National Treasure*, several parties seek to claim the wealth they anticipate the Declaration of Independence could reveal. However, that two-century-old document will only reveal its secret when viewed through the proper set of lenses. The Gospel of John, an even more ancient document, also requires a set of lenses crafted using elements from its own time period in order to reveal its hidden treasure. Ultimately, the appropriateness of any applied lens will be assessed by the clarity it provides the one actually reading the Gospel according to Saint John.

During the final editing of this book, a colleague posted on his social media platform a description epitomizing his experience reading the Fourth Gospel. I felt his comment a fitting postscript for this work, and asked his permission to quote it here. Perry Stepp, a New Testament scholar and now the president of the Biblical Institute of Zagreb in Croatia, wrote, the Gospel of John "is a riptide, an avalanche, the corona of lightning around a volcanic eruption. It's devastating. It's the richest and most powerful single piece of literature I have ever read."[8]

NOTES

1. John 9:37–41.
2. A classic demonstration is provided by R. E. Brown in the introduction of his commentary, *John* 29A:xxiv–xxxix.
3. The verses are applied to different editions as follows: v. 36b—2nd, v. 37—1st, vv. 38–42a—3rd, vv. 42b–45—2nd, vv. 46–50—3rd, von Wahlde, *Gospel of John*, 1:589.
4. Vv. 1–2—2nd, v. 3—3rd, v. 4—2nd, vv. 5–6—3rd, vv. 7–8—2nd, von Wahlde, *Gospel of John*, 1:597.
5. This conclusion is valid only for the sections examined in this study. Further analysis could be made by comparing the themes throughout the entire Gospel against von Wahlde's reconstruction.
6. Stan Harstine, *A History of the Two-Hundred-Year Scholarly Debate about the Purpose of the Prologue to the Gospel of John: How Does Our Understanding of the Prologue Affect Our Interpretation of the Subsequent Text?* (Lewiston, NY: Edwin Mellen, 2015), 95–97.

7. Stan Harstine, "A Helical Reading of the Fourth Gospel: A Prelude to the Prologue?" (paper, Southwest Commission on Religious Studies, Irving, TX, March 13, 2010), and *History*, 87. While researching for this volume I found that Jan G. van der Watt also discusses this spiral pattern in John's argumentation. Van der Watt, "Repetition and Functionality," 106–8. After completing this writing, I came across the work by John Breck, who utilizes this language with respect to various biblical books and more specifically in speaking about John 6. *The Shape of Biblical Language: Chiasmus in the Scriptures and Beyond* (Crestwood, NY: St Vladimir's Seminary Press, 1994), 183.

8. Perry L. Stepp, "Every time I dip my toe into the Gospel of John it sucks me in. GJn is a riptide, an avalanche, the corona of lightning around a volcanic eruption. It's devastating. It's the richest & most powerful single piece of literature I have ever read." Facebook, April 3, 2021.

Bibliography

Alter, Robert. *The Art of Biblical Narrative*. Basic Books, 1981.
Anderson, Paul N. "On Guessing Points and Naming Stars: Epistemological Origins of John's Christological Tensions." In *The Gospel of John and Christian Theology*, edited by Richard Bauckham and Carl Mosser, 311–45. Grand Rapids: Eerdmans, 2008.
Ando, Clifford. *Imperial Ideology and Provincial Loyalty in the Roman Empire*. Berkeley: University of California Press, 2000.
Ashton, John. "Really a Prologue?" In *The Prologue of John: Its Literary, Theological, and Philosophical Contexts. Papers Read at the Colloquim Ioanneum 2013*, edited by Jan G. van der Watt, R. Alan Culpepper, and Udo Schnelle, 27–44. Wissenschaftliche Untersuchungen Zum Neuen Testament 359. Tübingen: Mohr Siebeck, 2016.
Ashton, John. *Understanding the Fourth Gospel*. New York: Oxford University Press, 2007.
Athanasius. *Orations against the Arians*.
Attridge, Harold W. "Argumentation in John 5." In *Rhetorical Argumentation in Biblical Texts: Essays from the Lund 2000 Conference*, edited by Anders Eriksson, Thomas H. Olbricht, and Walter Übelacker, 188–99. Harrisburg, PA: Trinity Press International, 2002.
Attridge, Harold W. "Genre." In *How John Works: Storytelling in the Fourth Gospel*, edited by Douglas Estes and Ruth Sheridan, 7–22. Atlanta: SBL Press, 2017.
Attridge, Harold W. "Genre Bending in the Fourth Gospel." *Journal of Biblical Literature* 121, no. 1 (Spring 2002): 3–21.
Bampfylde, Gillian. "More Light on John XII 34." *Journal for the Study of the New Testament* 5, no. 17 (January 1983): 87–89.
Black, C. Clifton. *The Rhetoric of the Gospel: Theological Artistry in the Gospels and Acts*. Louisville: Westminster John Knox, 2013.
Black, C. Clifton. "'The Words That You Gave to Me I Have Given to Them': The Grandeur of Johannine Rhetoric." In *Exploring the Gospel of John: In Honor*

of D. Moody Smith, edited by R. Alan Culpepper and C. Clifton Black, 220–39. Louisville: Westminster John Knox, 1996.

Black, David Alan. "On the Style and Significance of John 17." *Criswell Theological Review* 3 (Fall 1988): 141–59.

Borgen, Peder. "Observations on the Targumic Character of the Prologue of John." *New Testament Studies* 16, no. 3 (April 1970): 288–95.

Borgen, Peder. "The Gospel of John and Hellenism: Some Observations." In *Exploring the Gospel of John: In Honor of D. Moody Smith*, edited by R. Alan Culpepper and C. Clifton Black, 98–123. Louisville: Westminster John Knox Press, 1996.

Borgen, Peder. *The Gospel of John: More Light from Philo, Paul and Archaeology: The Scriptures, Tradition, Settings, Meaning*. Supplements to Novum Testamentum 154. Leiden: Brill, 2014.

Boyarin, Daniel. "The Gospel of the *Memra*: Jewish Binitarianism and the Prologue to John." *Harvard Theological Review* 93, no. 3 (2001): 243–84.

Boyle, John L. "The Last Discourse (Jn 13, 13–16, 33) and Prayer (Jn 17): Some Observations on Their Unity and Development." *Biblica* 56, no. 2 (1975): 210–22.

Brant, Jo-Ann A. *John*. Paideia: Commentaries on the New Testament. Grand Rapids: Baker Academic, 2011.

Breck, John. *The Shape of Biblical Language: Chiasmus in the Scriptures and Beyond*. Crestwood, NY: St Vladimir's Seminary Press, 1994.

Brodie, Thomas L. *The Gospel According to John: A Literary and Theological Commentary*. New York: Oxford University Press, 1993.

Brown, Jeannine K. "Creation's Renewal in the Gospel of John." *Catholic Biblical Quarterly* 72, no. 2 (April 2010): 275–90.

Brown, Raymond E. *The Gospel According to John*. 2 vols. Anchor Bible. Garden City, NY: Doubleday, 1966–70.

Brown, Sherri. "Beginnings: Introducing the Narrative of the Word through the Prologue of John's Gospel." In *Come and Read: Interpretive Approaches to the Gospel of John*, edited by Alicia D. Myers and Lindsey S. Jodrey, 29–41. Interpreting Johannine Literature. Lanham: Fortress Press, 2020.

Brown, Sherri. "The Greeks: Jesus' Hour and the Weight of the World." In *Character Studies in the Fourth Gospel: Narrative Approaches to Seventy Figures in John*, edited by Steven A. Hunt, D. Francois Tolmie, and Ruben Zimmerman, 397–402. Wissenschaftliche Untersuchungen Zum Neuen Testament 314. Tübingen: Mohr Siebeck, 2013.

Bultmann, Rudolf Karl. *The Gospel of John: A Commentary*. Philadelphia: Westminster Press, 1971

Chilton, Bruce D. "John 12:34 and Targum Isaiah 52:13." *Novum Testamentum* 22, no. 2 (April 1980): 176–78.

Conway, Colleen M. *Men and Women in the Fourth Gospel: Gender and Johannine Characterization*. Society of Biblical Literature Dissertation Series 167. Atlanta: Society of Biblical Literature, 1999.

Culpepper, R. Alan. *Anatomy of the Fourth Gospel: A Study in Literary Design*. Philadelphia: Fortress Press, 1983.

Culpepper, R. Alan. "John 5:1–18: A Sample of Narrative-Critical Commentary." Translated by Jean-Daniel Kaestli. In *The Gospel of John as Literature: An Anthology of Twentieth-Century Perspectives*, edited by Mark W. G. Stibbe, 193–207. New Testament Tools and Studies 17. Leiden: Brill, 1993.

Culpepper, R. Alan. *The Gospel and Letters of John*. Interpreting Biblical Texts. Nashville: Abingdon, 1998.

Culpepper, R. Alan. "The Prologue as Theological Prolegomenon to the Gospel of John." In *The Prologue of John: Its Literary, Theological, and Philosophical Contexts. Papers Read at the Colloquim Ioanneum 2013*, edited by Jan G. van der Watt, R. Alan Culpepper, and Udo Schnelle, 3–26. Wissenschaftliche Untersuchungen Zum Neuen Testament 359. Tübingen: Mohr Siebeck, 2016.

Culpepper, R. Alan, and C. Clifton Black, eds. *Exploring the Gospel of John: In Honor of D. Moody Smith*. Louisville: Westminster John Knox Press, 1996.

Danker, Frederick W., Walter Bauer, William F. Arndt, and F. Wilbur Gingrich. *Greek-English Lexicon of the New Testament and Other Early Christian Literature* (BDAG). Chicago: University of Chicago Press, 2000.

De Boer, Martinus C. "The Original Prologue to the Gospel of John." *New Testament Studies* 61, no. 4 (October 2015): 448–67.

Deeks, David. "The Structure of the Fourth Gospel." *New Testament Studies* 15, no. 1 (October 1968): 107–29.

Dekker, Jim. "Generativity, Covenant Witness, and Jesus' Final Discourse." *Ex Auditu* 28 (2012): 147–59.

Dewey, Joanna, "The Gospel of John in Its Oral-Written Media World." In *Jesus in the Johannine Tradition*, edited by Robert T. Fortna and Tom Thatcher, 239–52. Louisville: Westminster John Knox Press, 2001.

Dodd, C. H. *The Interpretation of the Fourth Gospel*. New York: Cambridge University Press, 1968.

Engberg-Pedersen, Troels. "A Question of Genre: John 13–17 as *Paraklēsis*." In *The Gospel of John as Genre Mosaic*, edited by Kasper Bro Larsen, 283–302. Studia Aarhusiana Neotestamentica 3. Göttingen: Vandenhoeck & Ruprecht, 2015.

Erikson, Erik H. *Childhood and Society*. 2nd ed. New York: Norton, 1963.

Estes, Douglas. "Rhetorical *Peristaseis* (Circumstances) in the Prologue of John." In *The Gospel of John as Genre Mosaic*, edited by Kasper Bro Larsen, 191–207. Studia Aarhusiana Neotestamentica 3. Göttingen: Vandenhoeck & Ruprecht, 2015.

Estes, Douglas. "Time." In *How John Works: Storytelling in the Fourth Gospel*, edited by Douglas Estes and Ruth Sheridan, 41–57. Atlanta: SBL Press, 2016.

Estes, Douglas, and Ruth Sheridan, eds. *How John Works: Storytelling in the Fourth Gospel*. Atlanta: SBL Press, 2016.

Forbes, John. *The Symmetrical Structure of Scripture: The Principles of Scripture Parallelism Exemplified, in an analysis of the Decalogue, the Sermon on the Mount, and other Passages of the Sacred Writings*. Edinburgh, T & T Clark, 1854. https://archive.org/details/symmetricalstruc00forbiala/page/n3/mode/2up.

Forster, E.M. *Aspects of the Novel*. New York: Harcourt, Brace & World, 1927.

Fortna, Robert T., and Tom Thatcher, eds. *Jesus in Johannine Tradition*. Louisville: Westminster John Knox Press, 2001.

Freed, Edwin D. "Entry into Jerusalem in the Gospel of John." *Journal of Biblical Literature* 80, no. 4 (December 1961): 329–38.

Frey, Jörg. *The Glory of the Crucified One: Christology and Theology in the Gospel of John*. Translated by Wayne Coppins and Christoph Heilig. Baylor-Mohr Siebeck Studies in Early Christianity. Waco: Baylor University Press, 2018.

Gordley, Matthew. "The Johannine Prologue and Jewish Didactic Hymn Traditions: A New Case for Reading the Prologue as a Hymn." *Journal of Biblical Literature* 128, no. 4 (2009): 781–802.

Green, Joel B. *The Gospel of Luke*. New International Commentary on the New Testament. Grand Rapids: Eerdmans, 1997.

Gregory the Great, *Moralia*. Oxford: John Henry Parker and London: J. G. F. and J. Rivington, 1844. http://archive.org/details/moralsonbookofjo18greg/page/n5/mode/2up?view=theater.

Gruber, Margareta. "Die Zumutung der Gegenseitgkeit zur johanneischen Deutung des Todes Jesu anhand einer pragmatisch-intratextuellen Lektüre der Salbungsgeschichte Joh 12,1–8." In *The Death of Jesus in the Fourth Gospel*, edited by Gilbert van Belle, 647–60. Bibliotheca Ephemeridum Theologicarum Lovaniensium 200. Leuven: Leuven University Press, 2007.

Hale, Martha. "Paradigmatic Shift in Library and Information Science." In *Library and Information Science Research: Perspectives and Strategies for Improvement*, edited by C. R. McClure and P. Herndon. Norwood, NJ: Ablex Publishing Corp, 1991, 343.

Harner, Philip B. *Relation Analysis of the Fourth Gospel: A Study in Reader-Response Criticism*. Lewiston, NY: Edwin Mellen Press, 1993.

Harris, Elizabeth. *Prologue and Gospel: The Theology of the Fourth Evangelist*. Journal for the Study of the New Testament Supplement Series 107. Sheffield: Sheffield Academic Press, 1994.

Harstine, Stan. "A Helical Reading of the Fourth Gospel: A Prelude to the Prologue?" Paper presented at the Annual Meeting of the Southwest Commission on Religious Studies. Irving, TX, March 2010.

Harstine, Stan. *A History of the Two-Hundred-Year Scholarly Debate about the Purpose of the Prologue to the Gospel of John: How Does Our Understanding of the Prologue Affect Our Interpretation of the Subsequent Text?* Lewiston, NY: Edwin Mellen Press, 2015.

Harstine, Stan. *Moses as a Character in the Fourth Gospel: A Study of Ancient Reading Techniques*. Library of New Testament Studies 229. Sheffield: Sheffield Academic Press, 2002.

Harstine, Stan. "The Fourth Gospel's Characterization of God: A Rhetorical Perspective." In *Characters and Characterization in the Gospel of John*, edited by Christopher W. Skinner, 131–46. Library of New Testament Studies 461. London: Bloomsbury T & T Clark, 2013.

Hera, Marianus Pale. *Christology and Discipleship in John 17*. Wissenschaftliche Untersuchungen Zum Neuen Testament 2. Reihe 342. Tübingen: Mohr Siebeck, 2013.

Hitchcock, F. R. Montgomery. *A Fresh Study of the Fourth Gospel*. London: SPCK, 1911.

Holmes, Michael W., ed. *The Greek New Testament: SBL Edition*. Atlanta: SBL Press, 2010.
Holst, Robert. "The One Anointing of Jesus: Another Application of the Form-Critical Method." *Journal of Biblical Literature* 95, no. 3 (September 1976): 435–46.
Hunt, Steven A., D. Francois Tolmie, and Ruben Zimmerman, eds. *Character Studies in the Fourth Gospel: Narrative Approaches to Seventy Figures in John*. Wissenschaftliche Untersuchungen Zum Neuen Testament 314. Tübingen: Mohr Siebeck, 2013.
John Chrysostom. *Homiliae in Joannem*.
Käsemann, Ernst. *The Testament of Jesus: A Study of the Gospel of John in the Light of Chapter 17*. Translated by Gerhard Krodel. New Testament Library. Philadelphia: Fortress Press, 1978.
Keener, Craig S. *The Gospel of John: A Commentary*. 2 vols. Peabody, MA: Hendrickson, 2003.
Klinger, Jerzy. "Bethesda and the Universality of the Logos." *St Vladimir's Theological Quarterly* 27, no. 3 (1983): 169–85.
Larsen, Kasper Bro. "Plot." In *How John Works: Storytelling in the Fourth Gospel*, edited by Douglas Estes and Ruth Sheridan. Atlanta: SBL Press, 2016.
Larsen, Kasper Bro. *Recognizing the Stranger: Recognition Scenes in the Gospel of John*. Brill Interpretation Series 93. Leiden: Brill, 2008.
Larsen, Kasper Bro, ed. *The Gospel of John as Genre Mosaic*. Studia Aarhusiana Neotestamentica 3. Göttingen: Vandenhoeck & Ruprecht, 2015.
Larsen, Kasper Bro. "The Recognition Scenes and Epistemological Reciprocity in the Fourth Gospel." In *The Gospel of John as Genre Mosaic*, edited by Kasper Bro Larsen, 341–56. Studia Aarhusiana Neotestamentica 3. Göttingen: Vandenhoeck & Ruprecht, 2015.
Lee, Dorothy A. "Martha and Mary: Levels of Characterization in Luke and John." In *Characters and Characterization in the Gospel of John*, edited by Christopher W. Skinner, 197–220. Library of New Testament Studies 461. London: Bloomsbury T & T Clark, 2013.
Lee, Dorothy. "The Prologue and Jesus' Final Prayer." In *What We Have Heard from the Beginning: The Past, Present, and Future of Johannine Studies*, edited by Tom Thatcher, 229–31. Waco: Baylor University Press, 2007.
Lee, Dorothy A. *The Symbolic Narratives of the Fourth Gospel: The Interplay of Form and Meaning*. Sheffield: JSOT Press, 1994.
Liddell, Henry George, Robert Scott, and Henry Stuart Jones. *A Greek-English Lexicon*. 9th ed. Oxford: Clarendon Press, 1996.
Lightfoot, John B. *A Commentary on the New Testament from the Talmud and Hebraica*. 1658.
Lincoln, Andrew T. *The Gospel According to Saint John*. Black's New Testament Commentaries 4. London: Continuum, 2005.
Lincoln, Andrew T. *Truth on Trial: The Lawsuit Motif in the Fourth Gospel*. Peabody: Hendrickson, 2000.
Malatesta, Edward. "The Literary Structure of John 17." *Biblica* 52, no. 2 (1971): 190–214.

Malina, Bruce J. "What Is Prayer?" *The Bible Today* 18 (July 1980): 214–20.

Malina, Bruce J., and Richard L. Rohrbaugh. *Social-Science Commentary on the Gospel of John*. Minneapolis: Augsburg Fortress, 1998.

Maritz, Petrus. "The Glorious and Horrific Death of Jesus in John 17: Repetition and Variation of Imagery Related to John's Portrayal of the Crucifixion." In *The Death of Jesus in the Fourth Gospel*, edited by Gilbert van Belle, 693–710. Bibliotheca Ephemeridum Theologicarum Lovaniensium 200. Leuven, Belgium: Leuven University Press, 2007.

McNeil, Brian. "Quotation at John 12:34." *Novum Testamentum* 19, no. 1 (January 1977): 22–33.

Mealand, David L. "John 5 and the Limits of Rhetorical Criticism." In *Understanding Poets and Prophets: Essays in Honour of George Wishart Anderson*, edited by A. Graeme Auld, 258–72. Sheffield: JSOT Press, 1993.

Miller, Susan. "Mary (of Bethany): The Anointer of the Suffering Messiah." In *Character Studies in the Fourth Gospel: Narrative Approaches to Seventy Figures in John*, edited by Steven A. Hunt, D. Francois Tolmie, and Ruben Zimmerman, 473–86. Wissenschaftliche Untersuchungen Zum Neuen Testament 314. Tübingen: Mohr Siebeck, 2013.

Moloney, Francis J. *Signs and Shadows: Reading John 5–12*. Minneapolis: Fortress Press, 1996.

Morris, Leon. *The Gospel According to Matthew*. Pillar New Testament Commentary. Grand Rapids: Eerdmans, 1992.

Myers, Alicia D. *Characterizing Jesus: A Rhetorical Analysis on the Fourth Gospel's Use of Scripture in Its Presentation of Jesus*. Library of New Testament Studies 458. London: Bloomsbury T & T Clark, 2012.

Myers, Alicia D., and Lindsey S. Jodrey, eds. *Come and Read: Interpretive Approaches to the Gospel of John*. Interpreting Johannine Literature. Lanham: Fortress Academic, 2020.

Neyrey, Jerome H. *The Gospel of John*. New Cambridge Bible Commentary. Cambridge: Cambridge University Press, 2007.

Neyrey, Jerome H. *The Gospel of John in Cultural and Rhetorical Perspective*. Grand Rapids: Eerdmans, 2009.

North, Wendy E. S. *A Journey Round John: Tradition, Interpretation and Context in the Fourth Gospel*. Library of New Testament Studies 534. London: Bloomsbury T & T Clark, 2015.

North, Wendy E. S. "The Anointing in John 12.1–8: A Tale of Two Hypothesis." In *A Journey Round John: Tradition, Interpretation and Context in the Fourth Gospel*, 179–92. Library of New Testament Studies 534. London: Bloomsbury T & T Clark, 2015.

North, Wendy S. "'The Scripture' in John 17.12." In *A Journey Round John: Tradition, Interpretation and Context in the Fourth Gospel*, 45–56. Library of New Testament Studies 534. London: Bloomsbury T & T Clark, 2015.

O'Day, Gail R. "The Gospel of John: Reading the Incarnate Word." In *Jesus in the Johannine Tradition*, edited by Robert T. Fortna and Tom Thatcher, 25–32. Louisville: Westminster John Knox Press, 2001.

O'Grady, John F. "The Prologue and Chapter 17 of the Gospel of John." In *What We Have Heard from the Beginning: The Past, Present, and Future of Johannine Studies*, edited by Tom Thatcher, 215–28. Waco: Baylor University Press, 2007.

Painter, John. "Inclined to God: The Quest for Eternal Life—Bultmannian Hermeneutics and the Theology of the Fourth Gospel." In *Exploring the Gospel of John: In Honor of D. Moody Smith*, edited by R. Alan Culpepper and C. Clifton Black, 346–68. Louisville: Westminster John Knox Press, 1996.

Patterson, Steven J. "The Prologue to the Fourth Gospel and the World of Speculative Jewish Theology." In *Jesus in Johannine Tradition*, edited by Robert T. Fortna and Tom Thatcher, 323–32. Louisville: Westminster John Knox Press, 2001.

Petersen, Anders Klostergaard, "Generic Docetism: From the Synoptic Narrative Gospels to the Johannine Discursive Gospel." In *The Gospel of John as Genre Mosaic*, edited by Kasper Bro Larsen, 99–124. Studia Aarhusiana Neotestamentica 3. Göttingen: Vandenhoeck & Ruprecht, 2015.

Philo. *Allegorical Interpretation.*

Philo. *On the Cherubim.*

Power, Albert. "The Original Order of St. John's Gospel." *The Catholic Biblical Quarterly* 10, no. 4 (October 1948): 399–405.

Resseguie, James L. "Point of View." In *How John Works: Storytelling in the Fourth Gospel*, edited by Douglas Estes and Ruth Sheridan, 79–96. Atlanta: SBL Press, 2017.

Ridderbos, Herman N. "The Structure and Scope of the Prologue to the Gospel of John." *Novum Testamentum* 8, no. 2–4 (April–October 1966): 180–201.

Riley, Gregory. *The River of God*. San Francisco: HarperCollins, 2001.

Schnackenburg, Rudolf. *Das Johannesevangelium*. 3 vols. Herders theologischer Kommentar zum Neuen Testament 4. Freiburg: Herder, 1971–75.

Schnackenburg, Rudolf. *The Gospel According to St John*. 3 vols. Translated by Kevin Smyth, Cecily Hastings, Francis McDonagh, David Smith, Richard Foley, and G.A. Kon. New York: Seabury Press, 1980–82.

Schneiders, Sandra Marie. "Women in the Fourth Gospel." In *The Gospel of John as Literature: An Anthology of Twentieth-Century Perspectives*, edited by Mark W. G. Stibbe, 123–43. New Testament Tools and Studies 17. Leiden: Brill, 1993.

Sheppard, Beth M. "The Rise of Rome: The Emergence of a New Mode for Exploring the Fourth Gospel." *ATLA Summary of Proceedings* 57 (2003): 175–87.

Sheridan, Ruth. "John's Prologue as Exegetical Narrative." In *The Gospel of John as Genre Mosaic*, edited by Kasper Bro Larsen, 171–90. Studia Aarhusiana Neotestamentica 3. Göttingen: Vandenhoeck & Ruprecht, 2015.

Skinner, Christopher W., ed. *Characters and Characterization in the Gospel of John*. Library of New Testament Studies 461. London: Bloomsbury T & T Clark, 2013.

Skinner, Christopher W. *John and Thomas—Gospels in Conflict?: Johannine Characterization and the Thomas Question*. Princeton Theological Monograph Series 115. Eugene, OR: Wipf and Stock (Pickwick Pub), 2009.

Skinner, Christopher W. "Misunderstanding, Christology, and Johannine Characterization: Reading John's Characters through the Lens of the Prologue." In *Characters and Characterization in the Gospel of John*, edited by Christopher W.

Skinner, 111–27. Library of New Testament Studies 461. London: Bloomsbury T & T Clark, 2013.

Staley, Jeffrey Lloyd. "Stumbling in the Dark, Reaching for the Light: Reading Character in John 5 and 9." *Semeia* 53 (1991): 55–80.

Staley, Jeffrey Lloyd. "The Structure of John's Prologue: Its Implications for the Gospel's Narrative Structure." *The Catholic Biblical Quarterly* 48, no. 2 (April 1986): 241–64.

Stibbe, Mark W. G., ed. *The Gospel of John as Literature: An Anthology of Twentieth-Century Perspectives.* New Testament Tools and Studies 17. Leiden: E.J. Brill, 1993.

Stube, John C. *A Graeco-Roman Rhetorical Reading of the Farewell Discourse.* Library of New Testament Studies 309. London: T & T Clark, 2006.

Svärd, David. "John 12:1–8 as a Royal Anointing Scene." *The Gospel of John as Genre Mosaic*, edited by Kasper Bro Larsen, 249–68. Studia Aarhusiana Neotestamentica 3. Göttingen: Vandenhoeck & Ruprecht, 2015.

Tabb, Brian J. "Johannine Fulfillment of Scripture: Continuity and Escalation." *Bulletin for Biblical Research* 21, no. 4 (2011): 495–505.

Talbert, Charles H. "Artistry and Theology: An Analysis of the Architecture of Jn 1:19–5:47." *The Catholic Biblical Quarterly* 32, no. 3 (July 1970): 341–66.

Talbert, Charles H. *Reading John: A Literary and Theological Commentary on the Fourth Gospel and the Johannine Epistles.* Rev. ed. Reading the New Testament. Macon, GA: Smyth & Helwys, 2005.

Thomas, John Christopher. "'Stop Sinning Lest Something Worse Come upon You': The Man at the Pool in John 5." *Journal for the Study of the New Testament* 18, no. 59 (January 1996): 3–20.

Thompson, Marianne Meye. *John: A Commentary.* New Testament Library. Louisville: Westminster John Knox, 2015.

Thompson, Marianne Meye. "Light (phōs): The Philosophical Content of the Term and the Gospel of John." In *The Prologue of John: Its Literary, Theological, and Philosophical Contexts. Papers Read at the Colloquim Ioanneum 2013*, edited by Jan G. van der Watt, R. Alan Culpepper, and Udo Schnelle, 273–84. Wissenschaftliche Untersuchungen Zum Neuen Testament 359. Tübingen: Mohr Siebeck, 2016.

Turteltaub, Jon, dir. *National Treasure.* Burbank, CA: Walt Disney Pictures, 2004.

United Bible Societies. *The UBS Greek New Testament: Reader's Edition with Textual Notes.* Stuttgart: Deutsche Bibelgesellschaft, 2010.

Universität Münster, Institut für Neutestamentliche Textforschung. *Nestle-Aland Novum Testament Graece*, 28th ed. Peabody, MA: Hendrickson; Alban Books, 2018.

Van der Watt, Jan G. "Repetition and Functionality in the Gospel According to John: Some Initial Explorations." In *Repetitions and Variations in the Fourth Gospel: Style, Text, Interpretation*, eds. Gilbert van Belle, Michael Labahn, and Petrus Maritz, 87–108. Bibliotheca Ephemeridum Theologicarum Lovaniensium 223. Leuven: Peeters, 2009.

Van der Watt, Jan G. "The Composition of the Prologue of John's Gospel: The Historical Jesus Introducing Divine Grace." *The Westminster Theological Journal* 57, no. 2 (Fall 1995): 311–32.

Van der Watt, Jan G., R. Alan Culpepper, and Udo Schnelle, eds. *The Prologue of John: Its Literary, Theological, and Philosophical Contexts. Papers Read at the Colloquim Ioanneum 2013*. Wissenschaftliche Untersuchungen Zum Neuen Testament 2. Reihe 359. Tübingen: Mohr Siebeck, 2016.

Van Unnik, Willem Cornelis. "The Quotation from the Old Testament in John 12:34." *Novum Testamentum* 3, no. 3 (October 1959): 174–79.

Wahlde, Urban C. von. *The Gospel and Letters of John*. 3 vols. The Eerdmans Critical Commentary. Grand Rapids: Eerdmans, 2010.

Wahlde, Urban C. von. "The Pool(s) of Bethesda and the Healing in John 5: A Reappraisal of Research and of the Johannine Text." *Revue Biblique* 116, no. 1 (January 2009): 111–36.

Walker, William O, Jr. "The Lord's Prayer in Matthew and in John." *New Testament Studies* 28, no. 2 (April 1982): 237–56.

Watson, Francis. "Trinity and Community: A Reading of John 17." *International Journal of Systematic Theology* 1, no. 2 (July 1999): 168–84.

Westcott, Brooke Foss. *The Gospel According to St. John*. London: John Murray, 1896.

Williams, P. J. "Not the Prologue of John." *Journal for the Study of the New Testament* 33, no. 4 (June 2011): 375–86.

Wynn, Kerry H. "Johannine Healings and the Otherness of Disability." *Perspectives in Religious Studies* 34, no. 1 (Spring 2007): 61–75.

Author Index

Alter, Robert, 12, 14
Anderson, Paul N., 9
Ashton, John, 11, 15
Athanasius, 79
Attridge, Harold W., 84

Bampfylde, Gillian, 58–59
Black, C. Clifton, 62, 83
Black, David Alan, 77, 82
Borgen, Peder, 3n8, 40–41
Boyle, John L., 85
Brant, Jo-Ann A., 78, 82, 87
Breck, John, 110n7
Brodie, Thomas L., 60, 66, 80, 85, 91
Brown, Raymond E., 56–58, 61, 78, 85, 108n2
Brown, Sherri, 61n49, 62
Bultmann, Rudolf Karl, 9n53, 14–15, 41n13, 46, 56–57, 76, 79–80, 109

Chilton, Bruce D., 58
Conway, Colleen M., 60
Culpepper, R. Alan, 9, 10, 14

Deeks, David, 4, 8, 9n48
Dekker, Jim, 89–90
Dewey, Joanna, 12–13
Dodd, C. H., 57, 77, 89

Engberg-Pedersen, Troels, 87
Estes, Douglas, 5n21

Freed, Edwin D., 58
Frey, Jörg, 79–80, 82

Green, Joel B., 14n93
Gregory the Great, 1n2
Gruber, Margareta, 60–61

Harner, Philip B., 63
Harris, Elizabeth, 5, 10
Hera, Marianus Pale, 77, 79–80, 82, 86, 88
Hitchcock, F. R. Montgomery, 9n52
Holst, Robert, 57

John Chrysostom, 79

Käsemann, Ernst, 76, 79, 88n116
Keener, Craig S., 56–57, 61n49, 78n25, 79, 86, 88, 91

Larsen, Kasper Bro, 7, 14
Lee, Dorothy A., 60, 61n41, 61n48, 62, 91
Lincoln, Andrew T., 8, 46n52, 56–57, 61n49, 69, 76, 79, 82, 90

Malatesta, Edward, 77–78, 85–86
Malina, Bruce J., 13, 61n49, 87–88
Maritz, Petrus, 77–79, 82, 86, 91n142
McNeil, Brian, 58
Miller, Susan, 60–61
Moloney, Francis J., 61n49, 66, 69
Myers, Alicia D., 10, 44, 60

Neyrey, Jerome H., 62–63, 78
North, Wendy E. S., 91

O'Day, Gail R., 10
O'Grady, John, 86, 90–91

Painter, John, 10
Philo, 40–41

Rohrbaugh, Richard L., 13, 61n49

Schnackenburg, Rudolf, 4–5, 9, 56–58, 76–80, 88

Sheppard, Beth M., 86, 90
Sheridan, Ruth, 5
Skinner, Christopher W., 10, 14, 56
Staley, Jeffrey Lloyd, 10
Stube, John C., 2n3, 68n92, 87
Svärd, David, 60

Tabb, Brian J., 63
Talbert, Charles H., 10–11, 13, 42, 59–60
Thompson, Marianne Meye, 14, 81

Van der Watt, Jan G., 11, 110n7
Van Unnik, Willem Cornelis, 58

Wahlde, Urban C. von, 8, 76, 78, 109
Watson, Francis, 89
Westcott, Brooke Foss, 79

Scripture Index

Genesis
  1, 26
  1:1–5, 3
  1:2–3, 24
  1:5, 27
  2:2–3, 41
  3, 33

Exodus
  10:21–23, 25
  33, 40

Deuteronomy
  18, 105
  18–19, 67

Psalms
  61:7, 59
  88:37, 58
  91:11–12, 26

Isaiah
  40:3, 60

Matthew
  6:7–8, 78

John
  1:1, 13, 60, 84

  1:1–3, 11
  1:1–5, 3
  1:1–11, 50, 69
  1:1–18, 4, 8, 45, 85, 90
  1:3, 30
  1:4, 23, 29, 30, 35n25, 45
  1:5, 24, 67, 80
  1:6, 8
  1:6–7, 91
  1:8, 68
  1:9, 68
  1:11–18, 69
  1:12, 91
  1:14, 69, 79–80, 91, 91n142
  1:14–18, 86, 91
  1:16–18, 11
  1:17, 46
  1:18, 13, 69, 96
  1:19, 42, 46n59
  1:19–27, 60
  1:19–2:11, 42
  1:19–5:47, 11
  1:29, 84
  1:29–30, 11
  1:34, 26
  1:35–51, 7n35
  1:43–44, 61
  1–4, 4
  2, 82

2:1, 84
2:13–22, 42
2:23, 67
3:14–17, 31
3:15–16, 34
3:16–19, 50
3:17, 94
3:17–21, 33–34
3:18–21, 49
3:26–33, 46n61
3:34, 94
3:36, 31
4, 28
4:13–14, 30
4:19, 67
4:35–36, 46n52
4:43–44, 46n52
4:46–50, 30
4:53, 108
5:1–9, 42
5:1–16, 47
5:1–18, 42
5:1–30, 42
5:1–47, 40, 42
5:8, 47n63
5:10–18, 42
5:11, 47n63
5:12, 47n63
5:15, 42–43, 47n63
5:17–18, 47, 49
5:18, 40
5:19–30, 42–43, 47
5:19–47, 16, 42, 45, 49
5:21–26, 35
5:22–24, 94
5:23, 50
5:24, 32, 68
5:24–25, 29
5:31–47, 42–44, 48, 108–9
5:39, 32
5:41, 92
5:44, 79
5–20, 4
6, 29
6:1–59, 40

6:1–71, 59
6:1–11:57, 64
6:1–12:50, 11
6:2, 67
6:35–40, 64
6:40, 67
6:41–51, 64
6:52–59, 64–65
6:53–58, 29n16
6:60–69, 65
6:69, 7n35, 108
7, 28
7:3, 67
7:15–24, 40
7:16, 108
7:32–36, 65
8:12, 35
8:31–32, 32
8:31–54, 108
8:47, 65
8:51, 32, 68
8:51–55, 93
9:4–5, 25
9:38, 66
9:39, 67
10:7–10, 68
10:17–18, 92n149
10:54–12:43, 56
11:1, 56
11:1–12:11, 56, 60
11:1–12:36, 56
11:1–12:50, 56
11:9–10, 25
11:25–26, 31
11:27, 66
11:41–43, 60
11:42, 94n153
11:43, 31
11:54–12:19, 66
11:55–12:36, 56
12:1–19, 66
12:1–50, 16, 59
12:12, 80
12:13–15, 69
12:17, 58, 91

12:20–36, 66
12:24, 58
12:24–26, 68
12:27–28, 60, 86
12:27–36, 91
12:28, 69, 80
12:28–29, 62
12:31–50, 63
12:34, 58
12:35–36, 34
12:36–50, 67, 108–9
12:37–43, 67
12:37–50, 64
12:43, 69
12:44–45, 67
12:49–50, 69
12:50, 32, 60
13:1, 76, 80
13:1–12, 93
13:1–16:33, 91
13:6–11, 92
13:16, 92, 94–95
13:20, 92–95
13:21, 94–95
13:31–32, 80, 84
13:31–35, 87
13:31–17:36, 87n111
13:38, 94
13–17, 11
14:1, 92
14:6, 91, 93
14:10–12, 92
14:17, 92
14:19, 91
14:20, 95
14:24, 93
15:3, 92–93
15:7–17, 85
15:11, 85
15:18–25, 93
15:20, 92, 94–95
16:14–15, 92

16:20, 95
16:21, 58
16:23, 95
16:24, 92
16:27, 92
16:30, 93
17:1, 77n16, 80
17:1–3, 78
17:1–5, 91
17:1–8, 93, 108–9
17:1–21, 16
17:2, 79
17:3, 32, 34, 78–79, 88
17:4–8, 91
17:4–23, 85
17:5, 77, 80
17:6–8, 91, 93, 95
17:6–11, 88
17:9–19, 77, 85, 85n87, 93
17:12, 91
17:13, 85
17:13–14, 95
17:13–17, 86
17:18–20, 95
17:20, 95
17:20–22, 91
17:20–26, 93
17:21, 95
17:22, 95
17:24, 91
17:25, 96
17:25–26, 95
20:1–31, 4
20:28, 7n38
20:31, 8
21, 8

Romans
9, 26

1 John
5:20, 79

About the Author

Stan Harstine, Ph.D., teaches at Friends University in Wichita, Kansas. His academic work focuses on the Gospel of John and on ways this text is interpreted. He is the author of two additional volumes, *Moses as a Character in the Fourth Gospel* (Sheffield Academic Press, 2002) and *A History of the Two-Hundred-Year Scholarly Debate about the Purpose of the Prologue to the Gospel of John* (Edwin Mellen Press, 2015). Dr. Harstine has contributed chapters on characterization and on the prologue for edited volumes. He serves as an area editor for Christian Origins for the journal *Religious Studies Review*.

www.ingramcontent.com/pod-product-compliance
Lightning Source LLC
Chambersburg PA
CBHW021357300426
44114CB00012B/1271